# JOB SKILLS

## FOR THE 21ST CENTURY

### A GUIDE FOR STUDENTS

by

**LAWRENCE K. JONES**

Oryx Press
1996

The rare Arabian Oryx is believed to have inspired the myth of the unicorn. This desert antelope became virtually extinct in the early 1960s. At that time, several groups of international conservationists arranged to have 9 animals sent to the Phoenix Zoo to be the nucleus of a captive breeding herd. Today the Oryx population is nearly 1000, and over 500 have been returned to reserves in the Middle East.

Copyright © 1996 by The Oryx Press
4041 North Central at Indian School Road
Phoenix, Arizona 85012-3397

Published simultaneously in Canada

Printed and Bound in the United States of America

∞ The paper used in this publication meets the minimum requirements of American National Standard for Information Science – Permanence of Paper for Printed Library Materials, ANSI Z39.48, 1984.

**Library of Congress Cataloging-in-Publication Data**

Jones, Lawrence K.
    Job skills for the 21st century: a guide for students/
by Lawrence K. Jones.
        p. cm.
    Includes bibliographical references and index.
    ISBN 0-89774-956-1 (pbk.)
    1. Vocational guidance.  2. Labor demand—Forecasting.  3. Twenty-first century—Forecasts.  4. Students—Employment  I. Title.
HF5381.J654   1995                                                          95-42438
331.7'02—dc20                                                                   CIP

*To Jeanine, Mark, and Juliet*

# Contents

# Acknowledgments

This book is the work of many individuals. The contribution of Margaret Isenberg's second period class at Daniels Middle School goes at the top of the list. They read over the manuscript, tried out exercises, and discussed the strengths and weakness of the book in their teams. Their criticisms, praises, and suggestions for improvement were invaluable. Margaret made this and much more possible. Her "can do" spirit, creative energy, and outstanding teaching skills were an inspiration to me.

The Wake County Public Schools were most hospitable and helpful, in particular, the faculty and counselors and staff at Daniels Middle School, Enloe High School, and Cary High School.

I am fortunate to have, as my friend and walking partner, John Arnold, a nationally recognized authority on the middle school. His thoughtful, creative ideas were a great help.

Many outstanding teachers contributed to this book. They wrote the activities that follow the description of each of the Foundation Skills in Chapters 6, 7, 8, and 9. I was impressed, and I think you will be, with the exceptional quality of their ideas. I thank them for their inspired work.

I am indebted to the work done by the Secretary's Commission on Achieving Necessary Skills (SCANS) and their staff. I borrowed freely from their publications.

Taking the photographs for this book was a challenge. Many people helped. I want particularly to thank Mitchell Ward, Barbara Seeger Efird, Diane Lambeth, Phillip Watkins, Anita Stallings, Deborah Mangum, and John Geraghty. Patricia Denkler-Rainey contributed her own photographs for Chapter 12. Several organizations either contributed photographs, or helped obtain them: Campus Child Care Center (Rebecca Bowman), Siemens (Steven Morgan), *Black Issues in Higher Education* (William E. Cox), Wake Technical Community College (Karen Kornegay), Exide Electronics (Al Williams), Delta Air Lines (Patricia Frey), Durham Regional Hospital (Anne Doster), The Raleigh City Parks and Recreation Department (Wendy White and Dwayne Patterson), and TIAA-CREF (Claire Sheahan). My thanks to them all.

## THE INTERVIEWS

Although the interviews in this book are based on actual conversations, they were all edited for clarity, vocabulary, and length. Consequently, they should not be read as direct, verbatim quotations, even when quotation marks have been used.

# Foreword

## Why This Book Is Important for You

by James D. Burge

### WHY JOB SKILLS MATTER TO MOTOROLA

At my company, Motorola, the only constant is change. Jobs that were once relatively simple now require high-performance work processes and enhanced skills. Today's job skills, identified by Professor Lawrence Jones in *Job Skills for the 21st Century*, reflect these changing workplace realities and help students, job applicants, and employees anticipate change.

A couple decades ago, most factory jobs at Motorola were the classic short-cycle, repetitive work that required only high dexterity and a good work ethic. We really did not look for good communication skills or problem-solving skills, nor were we particularly interested in the applicant's ability to work constructively as a member of a team. As global competition became more intense, we at Motorola realized that we had to manage in a totally different way if we were to survive. We realized that our people, our human resources, held the key to our future success. We, therefore, committed to enhanced job skills for our current workforce and insisted that job applicants come well prepared with the job skills needed for a high-performance workplace.

Motorola has moved to a high-performance work organization that taps the resources of all employees as they move through a process of continuous improvement; decentralizes authority and responsibility by empowering employees to make decisions at the lowest possible level; expands jobs from repetitive, short-cycle tasks to an accountability for the entire process; opens lines of vertical and horizontal communication, and commits to the continuous education of employees to increase their problem-solving abilities and specific job skills.

Today the entry-level Motorola employee produces world-class products and assumes the following responsibilities:

Schedules work

Enters data and analyzes computer reports

Tracks inventory

Performs routine maintenance of sophisticated equipment

Analyzes manufacturing performance metrics and applies process control in the pursuit of Six Sigma Quality (virtual perfection)

Works on teams with technicians, engineers, and others to solve problems and improve the process

Deals directly with customers and vendors

Helps make equipment purchase decisions

Understands Motorola's competitive position

## WHAT ARE JOB SKILLS?

Job skills are the performance specifications that identify the knowledge, skills, and abilities (competencies) an individual needs to succeed in the workplace. Skills provide a common language of quality and expectations for everyone—students, employers, employees, job seekers, educators, and human resource managers.

*Job Skills for the 21st Century* references the work of the Secretary's Commission on Achieving Necessary Skills (SCANS); I served on that commission. SCANS focused on one important aspect of schooling: what we called the "learning a living" system. A high-performance (and high pay) workplace requires employees who have a solid foundation in the basic literacy and computational skills, in the thinking skills necessary to put knowledge to work, and in the personal qualities that make employees dedicated and trustworthy.

In industry today, where jobs are routinely re-engineered, where employees are changing jobs frequently, where training and education costs are rising, and where the pace of change is increasing dramatically, defined job skills help employers and employees gauge their own training and education skills.

*Job Skills for the 21st Century* will show you how your job skills are the key to success, and how you can build them to succeed in life.

*Jim Burge is corporate vice president and Motorola director, Government Affairs/Human Resources; he has responsibility for Motorola's human resource public policy. Burge served as a commissioner, by appointment of the secretary of labor, on the Secretary's Commission on Achieving Necessary Skills (SCANS), which has identified those workplace competencies needed by high school students to contribute effectively in a high-performance work environment. He has recently received a congressional appointment to the National Skill Standards Board, which will stimulate the development of national voluntary skill standards for broad-based occupational skills.*

# Foreword

by John Arnold

*Job Skills for the 21st Century* is a substantive and imaginative book that will have great appeal and benefit to students, as well as to their teachers and parents. In contrast to the usual impersonal, abstract, and tells-us-more-about-penguins-than-we-care-to-know textbook, *Job Skills* is personal, direct, and highly relevant to the needs and interests of adolescents.

Its content reflects Larry Jones's extensive and up-to-date knowledge of the world of work. In clear language, he makes a compelling case for the importance of job skills in today's competitive climate, elaborates the nature of the foundation and special skills involved, and shows how these skills can be developed.

A unique feature of the book is that a group of middle school students contributed significantly to it. Through frequent discussions with Jones, a class at Daniels Middle School in Raleigh, North Carolina, made numerous suggestions about content, vocabulary, and style. They then helped edit each chapter to make sure their ideas were properly expressed! As a result, the language, tone, and flow of the book are exceptionally user-friendly, and lend a delightful freshness to the text.

Practicing teachers have also made important contributions to *Job Skills*. A group of 16 experienced teachers, selected because of their capacity for innovative teaching, have designed some 142 activities to help students develop basic, critical thinking, interpersonal, and personal skills.

Thus the book is highly activity-oriented and practical; almost one-third is devoted to activities that engage students with the material. In addition to teacher-developed materials, Jones has designed or provided many inventories and checklists through which students can examine their personality characteristics and interests, assess their strengths and weaknesses relative to specific skills, compare their skills and interests with various job requirements, create career goals and plans, and develop a job skills portfolio.

Further, *Job Skills* has a real world focus, featuring numerous interviews, photographs, and portraits of people in the workplace. These workers speak directly to young people, telling the reader their backgrounds, and explaining the difficulties, challenges, and successes they met in the workplace.

This book does not back away from values; it squarely faces the facts of working life–that the playing field is not level, that many people, because of race, gender, or socioeconomic status, will have greater difficulties than others in developing skills or gaining meaningful employment. It consciously urges young people to take stands, to fight racism, sexism, and all attitudes and behaviors that denigrate others.

Finally, *Job Skills* is inspirational and optimistic. It urges young people to develop and pursue their dreams, to give their best whatever the circumstances. *Job Skills* advises young readers (1) to decide what they want and go for it, (2) to set goals and targets to reach, (3) to plan their future step by step, and (4) to work hard to reach their goals. Especially inspiring are the stories about people who have overcome obstacles to reach their dreams, including the first woman to land a plane on an aircraft carrier and an African-American man who has become CEO of the TIAA-CREF, the world's largest pension fund.

A clue to Jones's optimism and conviction about the importance of job skills may be found in his description of his own personal experiences.

> I grew up on a chicken farm in California. My mother and father struggled. . . . When I graduated from high school, I went to work as an office clerk. . . a boring, low-paying job. I lacked self-confidence. . . . Then my life changed. . . I got good jobs. . . I travel. . . have fun. . . own two homes. . . financed college educations. . . . How did this happen? . . . *Education* and *skills* made the difference.

The openness and genuineness with which Jones writes, coupled with his command of the field and knowledge of adolescence, makes *Job Skills for the 21st Century* highly readable and a unique and significant contribution to the field of career education.

*John Arnold is associate professor of Curriculum and Instruction and coordinator of Middle Grades Education at North Carolina State University. He has 35 years of experience as a middle school teacher, principal, and professor; has written four books and numerous articles about innovative teaching; and has served as a consultant to schools throughout the country, as well as to the National Board for Professional Teaching Standards and Nickelodeon Cable Television.*

# Introduction

This book is written for you if you are in your teen years. If you are in middle school or high school, I wrote this book for you. You will be working soon. These next few years will fly by. And what you do now will dramatically affect your future.

Your decisions today, and in the months ahead, will have a major impact on such questions as: Will I find a job? Will it be a good one? Who will be my friends? Will I be able to afford a car? Will I be able to get married?

The world of work is a constantly changing, challenging one. Competition. Unemployment. Low pay. Job hunting. What you do now will make a big difference in how you handle these challenges. This book will show you how to be strong, confident, and powerful. With hard, intelligent work you can excel. You can reach your dreams. This book will show you how your job skills are the key to success, and how you can build them to succeed in life.

This book is written for you if you are a concerned adult. You know how tough the work world can be for the unprepared. You know about the "working poor," nearly one-fifth of our full-time workforce who are unable to earn enough to get themselves above the poverty line. You know too about the millions of managers who have been laid off due to mergers and downsizing and about the loss of job security many workers are facing today. You also know that job skills are what really count in the workplace. With marketable job skills, you are in the driver's seat. You are powerful; the future is bright. This book will help you communicate this message to our youth. It describes what skills are, which ones are needed by workers, and how to learn them. It shows how to chart a career direction, set goals, and achieve them. You will find this book a valuable tool in helping young people reach their dreams.

PART one

# SKILLS: THE KEYS TO SUCCESS

# CHAPTER 1

# Working Together for Your Success

**I**t's great to feel strong, confident, and successful. To earn praise from friends and family. To feel powerful. To know that you control your own future. To be able to help your family and friends. The secret to achieving these goals? Skills! Skills make these things possible.

Skills are simply the things you learn to do. As a baby, you learned to walk and talk. Over the years you have learned many other skills—sports skills; reading, writing, and math skills; music or drama skills; and people skills. Whatever skills you have, don't they make life more fun and interesting? Don't they make you a happier person? Give you greater strength and confidence?

Skills are essential for success. Whether it is a satisfying marriage or friendship, raising children, owning nice clothes and a home, or living a life of adventure—they all require well-developed skills.

Skills are needed in most occupations. For example, bus drivers must learn to move their eyes, hands, and feet together to drive a bus safely through traffic. Likewise, chemists must learn to operate instruments to tell what chemicals make up a substance.

Skills lead to good jobs—after school, in the summer, or when you graduate. Skills lead to good pay so you can afford the car, clothes, or CDs you want. With a well-paying job, you can travel, buy a home, and have financial security for you and your family. Skills lead to jobs that are interesting and satisfying. *It makes no difference what your plans are after high school—work, college, the armed services, technical school—skills are essential for your success.*

## AN INVITATION

I invite you to join with me in learning about skills. It will be interesting and fun. You will learn the skills that lead to success. You will learn what you can do right now to be successful. You will hear what men and women say about their work. They will tell you about their jobs and give you their best advice. Together, we can launch you into the work world of the 21st century—where the skills you acquire now will help you be strong and take advantage of the best opportunities.

## LET'S GET ACQUAINTED

Since I will be your guide in this book, I want to share a bit of my life with you. I want you to know who I am and why I wrote this book.

I grew up on a small chicken farm in California. My mother and father struggled to make enough money to put food on the table. When I graduated from high school, I went to work as an office clerk. All day long I sorted papers—a boring, low-paying job. I lacked self-confidence and I was discouraged.

Then my life changed. I got good jobs. I traveled and taught in Great Britain, Germany, and Turkey. I have fun; I enjoy sailing, canoeing, camping, and music. My wife Jeanine and I own two homes. We financed college educations for our son and daughter.

How did this happen? What made the difference? Inheritance from Aunt Bessie? Lottery winnings? No. *Education* and *skills* made the difference.

My wife and I saved our money, planned ahead, worked hard, and *learned skills*. We learned to write, to speak in front of others, to work as members of a team, and to teach. We learned how to use a computer, do mathematics, and solve problems. Skills gave us the ability to do our jobs. Skills also made it possible to enjoy different hobbies and be good parents.

I wrote this book for you. In it you will learn

1. The foundation skills you need for every job.

2. How workers use their skills (they will tell you).

3. Interesting ways to learn these and other skills.

4. What skills you have right now.

5. How to choose your career direction.

## STUDENTS HELPED WRITE THIS BOOK

Students in middle and high school gave me valuable advice in writing this book. Students worked in teams and read over the chapters. They wrote down what they liked, didn't like, and ideas for making the book better. I met with the team captains at lunch to hear their ideas.

Margaret Isenberg explaining to her class how they will review the different chapters of this book.

One of the lunch meetings with the team captains. I'm writing down their comments about the book.

The students were doing the same work done by professional editors who work for publishers. They gave me many good ideas. One of the most valuable was their suggestion that I interview workers. They told me over and over again, "We want to know about the lives of real people. Things like, what do they like about their jobs? What is important to know?" So, I rewrote the book.

I interviewed men and women about their work. You will read their comments, starting with Chapter 2.

## GETTING STARTED

Keep these four points in mind:

1. *Many people want to help you.* Family members, including parents, grandparents, uncles, and aunts; teachers and counselors; ministers, priests, and rabbis; and

workers are eager to help you. Reach out to them. Talk with them about their jobs and ways to learn skills.

2. *Real learning requires action.* You can do interesting things to test the ideas in this book. For example, try out the activities I provide in this book. I guarantee you will find them challenging and eye-opening.

3. *You need to learn skills now to be ready for the future.* With the skills you learn this week, you will be more powerful next week. Brick by brick, skill by skill, you are building your future.

4. *It's up to you.* You owe it to yourself to be a skill learner. You will be more creative. Life will be more fun. You will better understand yourself and the world around you.

Promise to read this book and use its ideas. Set a goal. For example, "I will read at least one chapter each week, until I finish the book." Start today. Mark your calendar. Reward yourself each week when you've finished a chapter! Remember, "Today is the beginning of the rest of your life."

Vanessa Villalobos and Diego Soria enjoy science. They are working hard to learn the skills they need for the 21st century.

## THINGS YOU CAN DO

1. Talk with several adults you admire, and learn what they believe leads to success in work and life. Compare their answers. How are they similar? Different?

2. Relax and close your eyes and imagine your life 10 years from now. What will it be like when you wake up in the morning? As the day moves on? In the evening? On the weekends? Who will you be with? What will you do? Then, consider what skills you will need to achieve your dream. What can you do now as a step toward achieving your dream?

# CHAPTER 2

# The Challenge: Getting a Good Job

**G**etting a good job is a challenge.  Competition for good jobs is tough.

## YOUR COMPETITION IN OTHER COUNTRIES

If you are in Detroit designing cars for Ford, you are competing with automobile designers in Germany and Japan to see who can build the best car—the car that most people will buy.  The same is true for almost any other job.  You will be competing with workers in other countries to make the best product.

**Business-class trucks manufactured by Freightliner in North Carolina are driven aboard the M/V PACIFIC RIDER at the North Carolina State Ports Authority's Morehead City Terminal. The medium duty trucks were delivered to Ecuador and Chile.**
Photo courtesy of North Carolina State Ports Authority.

These trucks are being shipped to Ecuador and Chile to be sold. But will they sell? How will they compare in price and quality to trucks built in Korea, for example? The answer depends on which country has the best skilled workers.

## YOUR COMPETITION IN THIS COUNTRY

When hiring new workers, employers choose the person who has the best skills needed for the job. They choose among people like yourself. Some will be hired, some won't. You will want to have the best skills so that you are most likely to be hired.

In fact, if you plan ahead, you can have skills that are in great demand. Several companies may want to hire you! For example, there are more jobs today for physical therapists than there are people to fill them. Consequently, physical therapists have their pick of jobs.

### Competition Among Companies

The company you work for is competing against other companies. For example, Wendy's, Burger King, and McDonald's compete with each other for customers. The company that gets the most customers makes the most money. If you are working for McDonald's and McDonald's gets the most customers, you keep your job. If McDonald's gets the fewest customers, the company will have to cut costs by firing workers—you may lose your job.

In this competition, the company with the best product or service for the lowest price wins the most customers. To reach these goals, companies want to have the fewest workers possible. Workers who are not needed lose their jobs.

## The Gazelle and the Lion

I recently noticed a sign in the office of a large company. It quotes the company president and sends a powerful message.

> Our commitment to our customers must be ongoing and uninterrupted. Think about it this way: Every morning in Africa, a gazelle wakes up. It knows that it must run faster than the fastest lion or be killed. Every morning, a lion wakes up. It knows that it must outrun the slowest gazelle or starve.

> It doesn't matter whether you are a lion or a gazelle: When the sun comes up, you'd better be running. Our competitors who aren't running, who believe they can succeed without making a priority of service, simply won't last the decade.

This story describes the work world we live in today. What does it mean to you?

## MEET AL WILLIAMS

I want you to meet Al Williams. You can learn a lot from him. We talked at his office about his job, business competition, and skills. Al is in charge of training and development at Exide Electronics. He is an expert in job skills and a business leader.

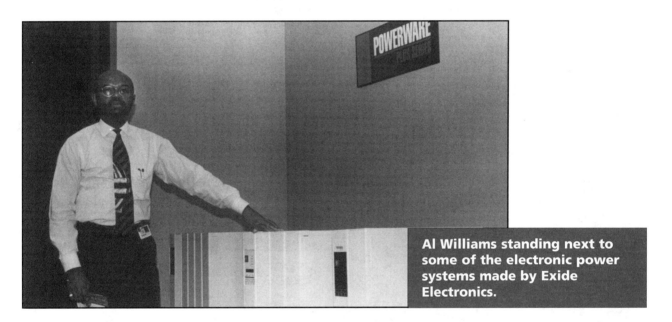

Al Williams standing next to some of the electronic power systems made by Exide Electronics.

LJ: To compete with other companies, are workers' skills important?

Al: Yes, absolutely. We need to have people take responsibility for their jobs and tasks. People must put aside the traditional approach of "I'll do what I'm told, and if they want me to change, they'll tell me." Or, when something goes wrong, someone says, "It's not my fault. He told me to do it." or "The supervisor told me to do it." We want workers to look for ways money can be saved, to anticipate problems, and to take responsibility.

We try to be cost-competitive. The people doing the work know best where the waste is. But they can't help if they don't have the necessary skills, like reading, writing, working in teams, making decisions—you name it. Unless you have those basic skills, you can't participate fully. For our company to compete, our people must have these skills.

## THE STAKES ARE HIGH

Without good job skills you will suffer. Period. You will be unable to get a good job and move on to other even better jobs.

Have you heard of the *working poor*? These are men and women, millions of them, who work hard, full time, but don't earn enough to stay out of poverty. They don't have the skills needed to get a well-paying job. It's a constant struggle for them to pay for food and rent. Often they have no medical insurance; they cannot afford to have a family doctor.

The drawing below by artist Ben MacNeill represents the working poor.

MacNeill says of the drawing,

I imagined it was late in the night and a tired woman has just come back from working at a clothing store where she is a clerk. Instead of sleep, however, a heated, whispered (so as not to wake the children) argument begins again with her husband over promises that are broken each month because the money they earn barely covers the bills, and nothing goes towards savings.

If you follow the tips in this book, you won't become one of the working poor.

And what about *unemployment*? Will you be asked to leave the company you are working for? Will you be unemployed? Yes, probably. Millions of Americans are unemployed each year. Sometimes a person's job skills become obsolete or they are replaced by a machine. People are laid off when businesses close or are purchased by other companies. Unemployment is nothing to be ashamed or afraid of. It's just one of those challenges of life that most of us are faced with.

Today, most people stay with their company an average of only four years. They are either laid off or decide to work for a different company. Most people become unemployed at some time in their working life, often several times.

What we are talking about here is *job security. Your job skills are your job security.* If you have good job skills, and you can learn new skills, you

- Are less likely to lose your job.

- Can find another job more easily, if you lose yours.

Palmer Watkins is a good example of how to handle unemployment. He has been laid off and has changed jobs several times. He has a positive outlook, and he has developed good sales skills that he can use in another job if he is laid off, or, if he decides he wants to work for someone else.

**Palmer Watkins holds one of the many lifting devices he sells. His strong sales skills give him job security.**

I asked Palmer about his sales skills.

Palmer: Sales skills are good marketable skills; there are lots of jobs in sales. You want to sell a product that interests you, that you can learn.

LJ:     What are your thoughts about getting laid off?

Palmer: Unless you are going to be something like a doctor or lawyer, you are going to have a lot of jobs; you're going to do a lot of things. There's nothing wrong with that. Don't think your present job is the last job you're ever going to have. Always be prepared. You may have to, or want to, leave your job for another one. Be ready.

LJ:     What about skills?

Palmer: Know what skills you have, and be prepared to brag about your skills. Don't be shy to do that. Be really proud of yourself and find those skills. Say what you're good at. If you are determined and hard-working, say so!

In this book, you will learn how to "find those skills." In Chapter 11 you will identify your "motivated skills." You will also learn how to "brag about yourself" in Chapter 16 when you develop your job skills portfolio.

## SKILLS AND THE HIGH COST OF LIVING

Your skills will have a big impact on what you can afford to pay for a car, rent for an apartment, tickets to a movie, CDs, and food—what we call your *cost of living*. Just how much does it cost to live? We will look at that first. Then, I will show you how this cost of living is related to skills.

### Cost of Living

What if someone offered you a job paying $6 an hour when you graduated from high school. Would you take it? That's $240 per week, about what you would earn as a cashier at McDonald's for 40 hours a week. Does that sound like a lot of money? Would it be enough to live on? Will $240 a week pay for your *cost of living*—your food, car payment, and housing? To answer this question, I have listed below the monthly expenses of a typical single person.

| | |
|---|---|
| Housing, renting an unfurnished apartment | $350 |
| Utilities (gas, electricity, water, garbage, and sewer) | $100 |
| Phone | $25 |
| Cable TV | $25 |
| Car payment (used, you owe $9,000 at 8% interest) | $220 |
| Car costs (license, insurance, maintenance, gas and oil) | $200 |
| Clothing | $125 |
| Food | $150 |
| Entertainment | $60 |
| Furnishings for apartment | $50 |
| Savings | $100 |
| Miscellaneous (gifts, pets, etc.) | $40 |
| TOTAL | $1445 |

It helps to think about this on a yearly basis, so let's multiply this figure by 12 months: 12 x $1,445 = $17,340. Now, let's figure out how much you would earn a year at $6 an hour. First, how many work hours are there in a year? There are 40 work hours in a week, times 52 weeks in a year for a total of 2,080 hours per year. Second, how much would you earn in a year? To determine this figure, multiply 2,080 by $6 for an answer of $12,480. This is your *gross pay*.

But, wait, this is not what you get! Your employer will deduct (subtract) from this $12,480 various amounts for taxes, Social Security, retirement, and medical insurance. Let's assume that these deductions amount to 20 percent. So, to calculate your *net pay* (what you actually take home), we multiply the $12,480 by .80 for a total of $9,984.

You can see that while $240 a week may sound like a lot of money, it won't come close to paying your expenses if they are anything like those in the example.

## HOW SKILLS ARE RELATED TO WHAT YOU EARN

Look at how much skills can earn for you.

| TYPE OF JOB | MEDIAN NET PAY |
|---|---|
| **UNSKILLED** *(less than one week of training)* | |
| Farm worker | $10,234 |
| Machine feeder | $13,021 |
| Hand packer | $11,565 |
| Assembler of small products | $14,227 |
| Carpenter's helper | $12,064 |
| **SEMISKILLED** *(three to six months of training)* | |
| Truck driver | $18,512 |
| Crane operator | $22,630 |
| Bus driver | $16,765 |
| Postal clerk | $25,459 |
| Security guard | $14,061 |
| Janitor | $12,605 |
| Sales counter clerk | $11,981 |
| Cashier | $9,402 |
| **SKILLED** *(college or technical school training)* | |
| Legal assistant | $22,298 |
| Electrician | $22,838 |
| Auto mechanic | $17,555 |
| Electrical or electronic technician | $24,586 |
| Health technologist or technician | $19,053 |
| Technical writer | $29,952 |
| Registered nurse | $28,579 |
| Chemist, biological scientist | $30,035 |
| Engineer | $37,898 |
| Doctor | $42,390 |
| Lawyer | $48,422 |

In summary, it costs a lot to live. Job skills are a major factor in determining the kind of life you live. If you have strong skills, you will earn more money and be able to live a more comfortable life.

## WORKERS LEARNING NEW SKILLS

You will learn new job skills throughout your life. Much of what you learn will be on the job. Richard Scott is a good example of on-the-job learning.

**Through on-the-job training, Richard Scott learns how to lay out sheet metal.**

Al Williams explained what Richard is learning.

When you are making punches in sheet metal, you have to be very, very accurate about the location of the hole, the cutout, or whatever indentation you are going to make. Richard is using mathematics to determine where to tell the machine to locate the hole on the sheet metal.

Not only does he need to consider the distance from point A to point B, but he also has to consider the thickness of the material. We may be talking about thousandths of an inch here, as opposed to tenths or eighths of an inch. He has to be very precise.

You will also learn skills off the job. We will end this chapter with the stories of two people who are doing just that.

Christine and Ted are taking a surveying course at Wake Technical Community College. Surveying is the process of determining the precise location of land and the features on that land, like hills and streams, trees, buildings, roads, and power lines. Surveying is needed when buildings, roads, and bridges are built.

Christine and Ted have worked for many years. They are upgrading their skills by learning surveying.

In the photograph, Christine and Ted are practicing their skill in using a theodolite, an instrument for measuring horizontal lines and vertical angles. Christine is in the Landscape Architecture Technology program. She was working in the field of landscaping, but the work was too strenuous for a person of her size, and she was injured. She had to find a job that was not as physically demanding. She decided to work in the design part of landscape work, rather than do the part that requires heavy and frequent lifting.

Ted is in the Surveying Technology program. He works full time and takes this course after work. Ted believes these new skills will increase his chances for promotion and better pay. "There are a number of people who will retire in the next few years, so I can fill their positions." His new surveying skills will also give him greater job security. "If I want to leave my job with the state, there are plenty of surveying companies that will hire me. I'll be in a much stronger position."

Just like Christine and Ted, you will be learning new job skills throughout your life. You are likely to

- Work on many jobs.

- Lose your job, perhaps several times.

- Quit your job for a better one.

- Change occupations.

What you do right now will make a big difference in just a few years. Goof off now, and you will suffer later. Work hard at strengthening your skills now, and you will have a much happier future.

## THINGS YOU CAN DO

1. Talk with adults you know, and ask them about job security. How secure is the job they have now? What do they believe affects their job security? How impor-

tant are job skills in keeping their jobs?  In finding a new job?  Do their skills affect how much they are paid?

2. Talk with adults who own their own business and ask them about competition from other companies.  Who competes with them?  What can a business do to succeed in this competition?

3. Talk with your parents about the costs of living.  Ask them to review the monthly costs that are listed in this chapter (p. 12).  Are these costs what you can expect?  Estimate what you think your monthly expenses will be for each item.

4. Discuss with your friends, parents, or teacher the story "The Gazelle and the Lion" found earlier in this chapter.  How does the story make you feel about going to work?  What steps can you take to prepare yourself?

# Skills, You Win—No Skills, You Lose

ost occupations require skills. Imagine, for example, that you are taking a trip with your grandmother. You need a motel room for the night. You decide to make reservations at the local Holiday Inn. Your grandmother has breathing problems so she must be in a room free of dust, pollen, and fumes. In addition, she uses a wheelchair, and needs a room that she can get to easily from the car. Now, you may be wondering, "How am I going to get a room that fits our needs?" You call Holiday Inn's 1-800 number, and you explain all of this to the reservation agent and she says, "Don't worry. I will connect you to our Guest Server's Representative. I am sure he can help you."

You hear, in a friendly voice, "This is James. How may I help you?"

You are now connected to James Benton, and he will help you. James is skilled in helping people with requests like these. He does it all the time; that is his job. I know because I met him at the Holiday Inn Worldwide Reservations Center. James is visually impaired; he has been blind from birth. In the interview below, you will learn about his job and the skills he uses.

James Benton gets information from the computer to help a customer with a special request.

LJ:     James, tell me about your job.

James:  I am a Guest Server's Representative.  I assist guests with special requests.  If guests have medical problems with, say, their backs or knees, I help them get a room on the first floor.  Sometimes I call resorts to make reservations.  In addition, I help train new reservation agents.  I take room reservations when we are busy.  I assist with the control room.  I am trained to do many of the jobs here; I fill in wherever I am needed.

LJ:     What did you do before this job?

James:  Before being promoted to my present job, I worked for three years on the reservation lines [he helped people reserve a room].  A technology teacher at Holiday Inn taught me how to do this using new computer technology.  I had eight days of training, and I was fully functioning in 14.

LJ:     James, you are very proud of how well you and the other visually impaired workers had done, aren't you?

James:  Yes.  We are ranked according to performance, and I was able to get up as high as number three [out of nearly 400 reservation agents].  My goal was to be number one, but Jack was able to claim the number one ranking, and Melissa ranked number two.

LJ:     James, you seem to be quite competitive.  Are you?

James:  You must learn to compete in a positive way early in life.  When I was in the Moorhead School for the Blind, we pushed each other.  We would challenge each other like "Let's see who can read this" or "I'm going to read six books, can you do as well?" Kids today don't do it as much as we did.  You just don't see it anymore; TV and video are distractions.  We went home to read a book, not watch a video.

In the job market the same thing applies.  You will always push forward, because you don't want the next guy or business to be better than you.  You will always respect them and appreciate their presence, but you need to be the best, to push forward. In school, you want to do your very best, to push yourself. You've got to start now, or you're going to be left behind; you're going to be at the mediocre end of the job market.

LJ: Is there much competition in the motel and hotel industry?

James: Yes, there is. We want always to be the best. We work hard to be the best.

Holiday Inn offers a lot of hotel products. You really need to know them well so you can sell them to your customers. For example, we have Holiday Inn Express Hotels, Crown Plaza Hotels, Crown Plaza Resorts, and Holiday Inn Select Hotels. You have to be familiar with all of them, and offer the best service to your customer.

LJ: How important are skills in your job?

James: Very important. Your skills need to be sharp. For example, you've got to have writing skills and computer skills. I'll be honest, I hated typing. It was the most difficult subject for me when I was in middle school. We had to learn punctuation, footnotes, term papers, letters, and so on.

At that point in your life, you don't think those kinds of skills are essential, but when you are out here in the world you find that computers drive the world. And you run a computer with a keyboard. The world is driven by the keyboard. You are in a lot of trouble if you don't know what a keyboard is. How are you going to run a computer if you can't type? You learn to type. To spell. To recognize good English, correct grammar. You need to be a good speller.

You also need to learn respect, how to act in a favorable way. People expect to be treated right. So you need strong people skills.

As you can see from this interview, James needs many skills to do his job well. He mentioned skills in writing, keyboarding, computers, and working with people. He also needs good problem-solving skills, skills in working with people from different backgrounds, and skills in teamwork. Without these skills, James would be unable to do his job. Without these skills, he would not have this job.

*Nearly all workers need skills to do their work. Whether you become a doctor, office manager, electronics technician, plumber, dancer, professor, or auto mechanic, you will need skills to do your job.*

## UNSKILLED OCCUPATIONS

Some jobs are called *unskilled occupations*. These are jobs that anyone can do once they are told how to do them. Examples are car washer, lawn mower operator, window cleaner, janitor, and garment folder. These kinds of jobs have two serious disadvantages for you. First, you will not earn enough money to meet your needs; life will be a constant financial struggle. You will find yourself among the working poor whom we discussed in the last chapter. Second, you can easily be replaced by some other person. There is little job security. After all, anyone can do your job. In this book, we will not consider unskilled occupations. When I talk about occupations, I am only talking about those that require skills.

## TWO TYPES OF SKILLS

Every occupation requires two types of skills:

1. Foundation Skills

2. Special Skills

Let's look at both of these types of skills.

## Foundation Skills

Foundation Skills are the skills that every worker needs—the ones you need to succeed. They are basic; they are the starting point. I have listed the Foundation Skills below.

### BASIC SKILLS

Reading

Writing

Mathematics

Speaking

Listening

### THINKING SKILLS

Creative Thinking

Problem Solving

Decision Making

Visualization

### PEOPLE SKILLS

Social

Negotiation

Leadership

Teamwork

Cultural Diversity

### PERSONAL QUALITIES

Self-Esteem

Self-Management

Responsibility

## Special Skills

These skills are called "special" because they are needed in some occupations, but not in all. You can see this in the work of a police officer. Let's take a look at six tasks police officers do.

1. Enforce traffic laws.

2. Give first aid at accidents.

3. Direct traffic around accidents and fires.

4. Investigate and write reports on the causes of accidents.

5. Arrest law violators.

6. Write daily activity reports.

What skills are needed to do these tasks? All of the Foundation Skills are needed—such as reading, writing, listening, decision making, teamwork, social skills, and visualization.

In addition, a police officer needs the following Special Skills:

1. Know the laws and regulations.

2. Know how to use guns and safety equipment skillfully.

3. Think clearly and react quickly in an emergency.

4. Know first aid and how to use it.

These skills are not needed in every occupation. They are "special" for certain occupations, like law enforcement.

## MARKETABLE SKILLS

You have many skills. For example, you probably know how to ride a bike. Would someone hire you to perform this skill? I can't think of many occupations that use this skill. Can you? Perform tricks in a circus? Deliver newspapers? Bike race competitively? Since few employers would pay you to ride a bike, we say that this skill is not marketable. In other words, you can't sell it to many employers.

*A skill is marketable when an employer will pay you to perform it.*

Think of the world of work as a big market, a labor market. You go to this labor market to sell your skills. You describe your skills on a piece of paper (called a resume) and send it to employers who you think may hire you. You fill out job applications and go for job interviews. Your hope is that you have the skills an employer wants and that the employer will buy your skills, that is, hire you.

Employers also go to the *labor market* when they have a job to fill. They put "Want to Hire" advertisements in the newspaper, and ask their friends and employees to tell others about the job openings. They interview people who apply. Then, they buy the skills they need by hiring the person who has those skills.

If you have skills employers need, you can sell them (get hired). If you don't have the skills needed, you do not get hired. Your skills are marketable when employers will pay you to perform them.

Now, let's put all this together. Foundation Skills are always marketable. Employers expect you to have them, and they will pay you to use them. In hiring, employers are also looking for people who have Special Skills, the ones needed for that particular occupation. So, you will want to have Foundation and Special Skills.

### Marketable Skills—A Conversation with Louise and Millard

To make this real for you, I want to share a conversation I had recently with Louise Kelly and Millard Arnold at the Exide Electronics plant. Louise supervises all the workers who do sheet metal fabrication for Exide. Millard is one of the workers in her department. He is a *computer numerical control operator,* or CNC operator.

In the next two photos you can see Millard working with his CNC machine. In the first photo, he is changing the cutting tools that this machine uses to cut sheet metal. In the second photo, you can see him entering numbers into the machine's computer. These numbers tell the computer how to cut the sheet metal precisely and automatically.

*In these photographs, you see Millard use highly paid, marketable skills.*

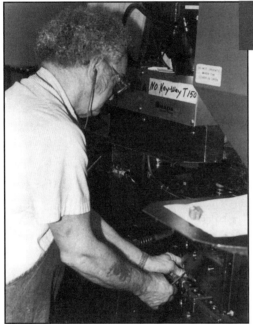

**Millard Arnold changes the cutting tools in the CNC machine.**

**Millard programs the CNC machine to cut the metal.**

Louise explained to me how her department works. The process begins with a drawing of a part; for example, a metal door for the cabinet that holds one of the power units. This drawing will show the height and width of the door and where various holes are located. The CNC operators take the information from this drawing and enter it into a computer. For example, they tell the computer what diameter the hole is for the door handle, and where it is located on the piece of metal.

When the CNC operator is ready to have the machine cut this door out of a piece of sheet metal, he or she first has to be sure the machine has the kinds of cutting tools that it needs to put a hole or cutout in the door. In the first photo, you saw Millard putting the correct cutting tools in the machine. Then Millard enters the information that the machine's computer needs to know, pushes a button, and the holes and cutouts are cut precisely in seconds.

I asked Millard if knowing how to run the CNC machine is a skill that gives him job security.

"Yes, it certainly does. It's a good skill to have. There is a lot of demand out there in the job market for people who have these skills."

Louise strongly agreed. She told me that recently two of her CNC operators quit to take jobs with other companies that paid more. It took her several weeks to find people to replace them, and she only got two job applicants.

Being able to operate a CNC machine is a good example, then, of a marketable skill. If you have the Foundation Skills and Special Skills, like those of a CNC operator, you will have no difficulty getting a job that pays well. In fact, your skills may be so valuable, that you will have employers coming to you, wanting to hire you.

If you are interested in learning more about the training to operate CNC machines, read the interview with John and Jerry in Chapter 15 (p. 182).

## SUMMARY

- An occupation is a set of tasks a worker performs.

- These tasks require skills in order to be done successfully.

- Every occupation requires both Foundation Skills and a certain set of Special Skills.

- Marketable skills are skills employers will pay you to perform.

- Workers with marketable skills are paid more, are less likely to be fired or laid off, are better able to find other jobs, and receive more raises and promotions.

In the next two chapters, we will take a closer look at the two types of skills. In Chapter 4, you will learn about Foundation Skills. In Chapter 5, we will explore Special Skills.

## THINGS YOU CAN DO

1. Read and do activity #4 at the end of Chapter 4. You will interview a person about his or her work to learn what skills are used. It's a great way to learn about job skills. Discuss how you can do it with your parents, teacher, or school counselor.

2. Survey the adults you know and ask them what they believe are their three most marketable skills. Be prepared to describe what a marketable skill is and to give examples. Keep a record of what skills they mention. When you finish your survey, check to see what percent of these skills are Foundation Skills and what percent are Special Skills.

# Foundation Skills

**W**hat skills do you need to succeed in the world of work? Several government commissions have worked hard to answer this question. For example, one is called the Secretary of Labor's Commission on Achieving Necessary Skills. I have used their work to create the Foundation Skills. *These are the skills needed by all workers* whether they are nuclear physicists, real estate agents, airplane mechanics, or auto assemblers.

When I showed the Foundation Skills to Lu Ann Herring, a bank vice-president for sales and service, she said: "This is excellent, wonderful! These are the types of things we really try to instill in our managers. These are just the basic skills that you need to succeed in business, like recognizing and complimenting your staff. Problem solving is really needed; negotiation . . . . I love this!"

Take a few minutes now and read through the Foundation Skills. In chapters 6, 7, 8, and 9 we will take a closer look at them.

## FOUNDATION SKILLS

### Basic Skills

**Reading:** Identify relevant facts; locate information in books/manuals; find meaning of unknown words; judge accuracy of reports; use computer to find information.

**Writing:** Write ideas completely and accurately in letters and reports with proper grammar, spelling, and punctuation; use computer to communicate information.

**Mathematics:** Use numbers, fractions, and percentages to solve problems; use tables, graphs, and charts; use computer to enter, retrieve, change, and communicate numerical information.

**Speaking:** Speak clearly; select language, tone of voice, and gestures appropriate to audience.

**Listening:** Listen carefully to what person says, noting tone of voice and body language; respond in a way that shows understanding of what is said.

### Thinking Skills

**Creative Thinking:** Use imagination freely, combining ideas or information in new ways; make connections between ideas that seem unrelated.

**Problem Solving:** Recognize problem; identify why it is a problem; create and implement a solution; watch to see how well solution works; revise as needed.

**Decision Making:** Identify goal; generate alternatives and gather information about them; weigh pros and cons; choose best alternative; plan how to carry out choice.

**Visualization:** Imagine building, object, or system by looking at a blueprint or drawing.

### People Skills

**Social:** Show understanding, friendliness, and respect for feelings of others; assert oneself when appropriate; take an interest in what people say and why they think and act as they do.

**Negotiation:** Identify common goals among different parties; clearly present your position; understand other party's position; examine possible options; make reasonable compromises.

**Leadership:** Communicate thoughts and feelings to justify a position; encourage or convince others; make positive use of rules or values; demonstrate ability to have others believe in and trust you because of your competence and honesty.

**Teamwork:** Contribute to group with ideas and effort; do own share of work; encourage team members; resolve differences for benefit of the team; responsibly challenge existing procedures, policies, or authorities.

**Cultural Diversity:** Work well with people having different ethnic, social, or educational backgrounds; understand the cultural differences of different groups; help people in these groups make cultural adjustments when necessary.

### Personal Qualities

**Self-Esteem:** Understand how beliefs affect how a person feels and acts; "listen" and identify irrational or harmful beliefs you may have; and understand how to change them when they occur.

**Self-Management:** Assess own knowledge and skills accurately; set specific, realistic personal goals; monitor progress toward goal.

**Responsibility:** Work hard to reach goals, even if task is unpleasant; do quality work; display high standard of attendance, honesty, energy, and optimism.

## SUMMARY

The Foundation Skills are the skills you need for the jobs of today and tomorrow. They are needed for all jobs. We will take a closer look at them in Chapters 6, 7, 8, and 9. In the next chapter, we will look at the Special Skills.

## THINGS YOU CAN DO

1. Is the meaning of any of the Foundation Skills unclear to you? Why not look them up in Chapters 6, 7, 8, and 9? In these chapters, real workers will talk about how they use these skills.

2. Show the Foundation Skills to workers you know, and ask them if they agree that these skills are needed. Which ones do they think are particularly important? Are there skills that they would add to this list?

3. Photocopy the Foundation Skills listed earlier in this chapter. Put the list in a place where it will remind you of these skills, such as on the wall next to the place where you study.

## INTERVIEWING WORKERS

A great project for a class or student group, or for you to do with a friend, is to interview workers to discover which Foundation Skills they use at work. Wouldn't it be interesting to talk with an engineer, social worker, pilot, truck driver, or veterinarian? To learn whether skills like teamwork or problem solving are important in their work? How these skills are used? You would be doing interviews just like the ones in this book.

Even better, why not create a program to share what you learn with other students in your class or school? Or students in the lower grades? Why not have the whole project broadcast on your local TV station? All these things have been done with great success at other schools. Why not talk about it with your teachers or the leader of your youth group? Not only will you learn a lot about work and skills, you will also strengthen your Foundation Skills because you will use all of them doing the project.

I will give you the basic information you need to get started. You can then go from there. You can make it as simple or as elaborate as you want. I will assume that you will be doing this as a class or youth group, but remember, you can simplify it and do it with a friend.

1. Develop a team approach. Your "team" would be your class or youth group.

2. Consider involving others. Organizations like Junior Achievement, the chamber of commerce, and vocational clubs at your school may provide valuable help. Talk with your school counselor to see what ideas he or she has.

3. Plan out such things as:

    a. Which occupations you want to interview. Be sure to get a variety, perhaps equal numbers from each of the six Holland personality categories (see Chapter 5).

b. How you will contact workers. You might want to ask your chamber of commerce for help. Or, writing letters works well.

c. Transportation, communication with parents (including permission).

d. How you will do the interview. I recommend that you do it in pairs: one of you asks the questions, the other takes notes; then, with the next interview, rotate your jobs. Be sure to practice beforehand.

e. Over what period of time the interviews will be done (preferably a week or less), and approximately how long each interview will last (e.g., 20 minutes).

f. Research about the occupation. You will get the most from the interview if you learn about the occupation first. For example, read about it in the *Occupational Outlook Handbook,* or a similar book, and complete an "Occupational Profile" from Chapter 10. Learn as much as you can about the skills that are used in the occupation.

g. How many workers each pair interviews (probably not more than four).

4. Communicate what you learn to others. You will be surprised and pleased to see how interested people are in what you discovered. Parents, teachers, businesspeople, and other students are interested in this topic.

a. Why not make a videotape that shows what you learned, then show it to interested groups? Many student groups have done this and really enjoyed it.

b. Why not present your findings to other students? For example, in many high schools, student teams went to middle schools to share what they learned. Or, for example, if you are in eighth grade, why not give a presentation to other students your age?

c. Why not involve your local TV station? In the past, they have shown a lot of interest in these projects. In addition to broadcasting what you do, they can give you technical advice on how to make videotapes.

5. Be sure to write a thank you note to the person when you are finished.

The next few pages contain a form you can use to conduct your job interview. It's a good idea to give the form to the person you are interviewing ahead of time, but ask them not to fill it out until you are there.

FOUNDATION SKILLS

# JOB INTERVIEW FORM

NAME OF INTERVIEWER _____

NAME OF NOTE-TAKER _____

DATE OF INTERVIEW _____

## INTRODUCTION

Introduce yourself and explain the purpose of the interview (to learn about job skills). Explain that the interview has four steps:

1. Getting information about the person being interviewed

2. Identifying this person's job duties

3. Rating which job skills the person uses

4. Learning how four of these skills are used

## STEP 1: GETTING INFORMATION ABOUT THE PERSON

Name _____

Organization or Company _____

Job Title _____

Phone Number _____

## STEP 2: GETTING INFORMATION ABOUT HIS OR HER JOB

What are the primary job duties involved?  In one sentence:

1. _____
   _____

2. _____
   _____

3. _____
   _____

4. _____
   _____

5. _____
   _____

## Step 3: Rating which Skills Are Used

Explain that you want to have the person rate each of the 17 Foundation Skills, based on their importance for his or her job. Mention that the skills are grouped into four categories: Basic Skills, Thinking Skills, People Skills, and Personal Qualities. You will read off each skill and ask the person to rate it on the scale below:

| | | | | |
|---|---|---|---|---|
| 0 | 1 | 2 | 3 | 4 |
| Not Important | | Important | | Very Important |

Give the person a copy of the scale. Write his or her rating on the line to the left of each skill.

## Basic Skills

_____ *Reading:* Identify relevant facts; locate information in books/manuals; find meaning of unknown words; judge accuracy of reports; use computer to find information.

_____ *Writing:* Write ideas completely and accurately in letters and reports with proper grammar, spelling, and punctuation; use computer to communicate information.

_____ *Mathematics:* Use numbers, fractions, and percentages to solve problems; use tables, graphs, and charts; use computer to enter, retrieve, change, and communicate numerical information.

_____ *Speaking:* Speak clearly; select language, tone of voice, and gestures appropriate to audience.

_____ *Listening:* Listen carefully to what person says, noting tone of voice and body language; respond in a way that shows understanding of what is said.

## Thinking Skills

_____ *Creative Thinking:* Use imagination freely, combining ideas or information in new ways; make connections between ideas that seem unrelated.

_____ *Problem Solving:* Recognize problem; identify why it is a problem; create and implement a solution; watch to see how well it works; revise as needed.

_____ *Decision Making:* Identify goal; generate alternatives and gather information about them; weigh pros and cons; choose best alternative; plan how to carry out choice.

_____ *Visualization:* Imagine building, object, or system by looking at a blueprint or drawing.

## People Skills

_____ *Social:* Show understanding, friendliness, and respect for feelings of others; assert oneself when appropriate; take an interest in what people say and why they think and act as they do.

_____ *Negotiation:* Identify common goals among different parties; clearly present your position; understand other party's position; examine possible options; make reasonable compromises.

_____ *Leadership:* Communicate thoughts and feelings to justify a position; encourage or convince others; make positive use of rules or values; demonstrate ability to have others believe in and trust you because of your competence and honesty.

_____ *Teamwork:* Contribute to group with ideas and effort; do own share of work; encourage team members; resolve differences for benefit of the team; responsibly challenge existing procedures, policies, or authorities.

_____ *Cultural Diversity:* Work well with people having different ethnic, social, or educational backgrounds; understand the cultural differences of different groups; help people in these groups make cultural adjustments when necessary.

## Personal Qualities

_____ *Self-Esteem:* Understand how beliefs affect how a person feels and acts; "listen" and identify irrational or harmful beliefs you may have; and understand how to change them when they occur.

_____ *Self-Management:* Assess own knowledge and skills accurately; set specific, realistic personal goals; monitor progress toward goals.

_____ *Responsibility:* Work hard to reach goals, even if task is unpleasant; do quality work; display high standard of attendance, honesty, energy, and optimism.

### STEP 4: LEARNING HOW FOUR OF THESE SKILLS ARE USED

1. Explain that you are now going to ask the person to talk about four different skills. You are going to choose one skill from each of the four groups.

2. Look over the ratings your person has given for the Basic Skills. Choose the one that seems most important.

3. Ask the person to give an example of how he or she uses this skill at work. Ask the person to describe a task where this skill is used.

4. Do the same thing with three other skills, one from each skill group.

Skill from Basic Skills group: _____

Description of task (one sentence): _____

_____

How skill is used to perform task: _____

_____

_____
_____
_____
_____
_____
_____
_____
_____

Skill from Thinking Skills group:_____

Description of task (one sentence): _____
_____

How skill is used to perform task: _____
_____
_____
_____
_____
_____
_____
_____
_____

Skill from People Skills group:_____

Description of task (one sentence): _____
_____

How skill is used to perform task: _____
_____
_____
_____
_____
_____
_____
_____
_____

Skill from Personal Qualities group: _____

Description of task (one sentence): _____
_____

How skill is used to perform task: _____
_____
_____
_____

# CHAPTER 5

## Special Skills and Occupations

**I**magine how astonished people 100 years ago would be to see all the interesting things that we can learn today. For example, just think of all the opportunities you and I have to learn skills in the creative arts. We can learn to play a flute, dance ballet, paint landscapes, blow glass, act in dramas, create jewelry, and design clothing. Think of the opportunities to learn in such areas as sports, science, cars, computers, finance, and photography. We can learn these skills through school courses, clubs, TV, books, videos, CDs, correspondence courses, volunteer work, camps, workshops, apprenticeships, and internships. It's a great time to be alive!

Because there are so many skills, it is a challenge to choose which ones to learn, which occupational field to prepare for. You want to learn the Foundation Skills, but which Special Skills do you want to learn? What will your career direction be? There are so many possibilities! In this chapter, I will show you a great way to start.

### FINDING OCCUPATIONS THAT FIT YOU

One way to decide on a career direction is to examine your traits—your interests, values, and abilities—and see which occupations fit them. This method is used by most school and career counselors, and we will use it in this chapter.

A psychologist named John Holland invented the following six personality types:

REALISTIC                INVESTIGATIVE               ARTISTIC
SOCIAL                   ENTERPRISING                CONVENTIONAL

Each personality type has a unique combination of interests, values, and abilities.  For example, Artistic people prefer activities that allow them to express ideas or feelings through dance, drama, music, writing, or craft arts.  They have artistic abilities, and they value the creative arts.

These six personality types can be used to group occupations.  For example, there are many occupations that can be grouped under the Artistic category, like writer, art teacher, disk jockey, and musician.

Isn't that great?!  If you know the personality type you are most like, you can identify occupations that might fit you.

What we want to do, then, is to find out which of the six personality types you are most like.  Once you know this, you can easily see which occupations are grouped with your type.  Let's get started.

## WHICH PERSONALITY TYPES ARE MOST LIKE YOU?

Are you primarily a Social person, or perhaps Realistic-Investigative?  We will investigate that now.

First, take out a piece of paper and make an answer sheet, like the one on page 37 (or you can photocopy it).

To what extent does each statement below describe you?  Rate each one using the scale shown below.  Write the number on your answer sheet.

| 0 | 1 | 2 | 3 | 4 |
|---|---|---|---|---|
| NOT TRUE OF ME | | SOMEWHAT TRUE OF ME | | VERY TRUE OF ME |

## REALISTIC

**a.** I prefer to work with things you can see and touch, like animals, objects, tools, or machines.

**b.** I generally avoid activities like teaching, giving help to others, or giving information.

**c.** I have abilities in working with objects, animals, and machines.

**d.** I do not have many abilities in teaching, counseling, or curing people.

**e.** Money or power are important to me.

**f.** I see myself as practical, frank, and hard-headed.

## INVESTIGATIVE

**a.** I prefer activities that involve precise observation, thinking, and study to solve mathematical and science problems.

**b.** I tend to avoid leading, selling, or persuading other people.

**c.** I have abilities for solving social, scientific, and mathematical problems.

**d.** I do not have many abilities in organizing or persuading others.

**e.** Adding to our knowledge about life is important to me.

**f.** I see myself as analytical, critical, and intellectual.

## SOCIAL

**a.** I like activities where I can help people, such as through teaching, first aid, or giving information.

**b.** I prefer not to work where I must use machines, tools, or animals to reach a goal.

**c.** I have abilities in areas like teaching, curing, developing, or informing.

**d.** I do not have many abilities in using tools, machines, or working with animals.

**e.** Social problems are important to me.

**f.** I see myself as helpful, friendly, and responsible.

## ENTERPRISING

**a.** I enjoy leading, selling, or persuading people to earn money or meet the goals of an organization.

**b.** I normally avoid activities that require careful observation and scientific thinking.

**c.** I have abilities in leading and persuading people.

**d.** I do not have many scientific and mathematical abilities.

**e.** Success in managing or selling is important to me.

**f.** I see myself as energetic, ambitious, and sociable.

SKILLS: THE KEYS TO SUCCESS

## ARTISTIC

**a.** I prefer activities that allow me to express my ideas and feelings in a creative way through art, drama, crafts, dance, music, or writing.

**b.** I usually avoid highly ordered or repetitive activities.

**c.** I have artistic and creative abilities that I can use in such areas as drama, music, or art.

**d.** I do not have many bookkeeping or clerical abilities.

**e.** The creative arts are important to me.

**f.** I see myself as expressive, original, and independent.

## CONVENTIONAL

**a.** I prefer working with numbers, records, or machines in a set, orderly way.

**b.** I prefer not to do vague, unstructured activities.

**c.** I have computing, clerical, or business abilities that I can use in working with written records and numbers in a systematic, orderly way.

**d.** I do not have many creative or artistic abilities.

**e.** I value success in business.

**f.** I see myself as careful, orderly, and conscientious.

**Name**_____ **Date**_____

## REALISTIC

A. ____

B. ____

C. ____

D. ____

E. ____

F. ____

**TOTAL** ____

## INVESTIGATIVE

A. ____

B. ____

C. ____

D. ____

E. ____

F. ____

**TOTAL** ____

## ARTISTIC

A. ____

B. ____

C. ____

D. ____

E. ____

F. ____

**TOTAL** ____

## SOCIAL

A. ____

B. ____

C. ____

D. ____

E. ____

F. ____

**TOTAL** ____

## ENTERPRISING

A. ____

B. ____

C. ____

D. ____

E. ____

F. ____

**TOTAL** ____

## CONVENTIONAL

A. ____

B. ____

C. ____

D. ____

E. ____

F. ____

**TOTAL** ____

Add up the numbers for each of the personality types on your answer sheet, and write the result where it says "Total."

Which type(s) do you have the highest scores for? Which type(s) are you most like?

Are any of your top scores tied? That's fine. Just read over the descriptions for the types and decide which one is most like you.

## IDENTIFYING OCCUPATIONS

Now look up the occupations listed for the type(s) you are most like in the following pages. For example, if you resemble the Social type, turn to that section to identify appealing occupations. Go ahead and get started. Write down on a piece of paper those occupations that appeal to you.

By the way, you will see groups of numbers in brackets, like [03.01]; ignore them for now. I will tell you how to use them at the end of the chapter.

## REALISTIC

### PLANTS AND ANIMALS [03.01, 03.02, 03.03, 03.04]

| | | |
|---|---|---|
| Animal Breeder | Farm Manager | Landscape Gardener |
| Animal Trainer | Forester | Nursery Manager |
| Dog Groomer | Greenskeeper | Vegetable Farming Supervisor |
| Farmer | Livestock Rancher | |

### SAFETY AND LAW ENFORCEMENT [04.01, 04.02]

| | | |
|---|---|---|
| Detective | Narcotics Investigator | Police Officer |
| Fire Chief | Park Ranger | Park Superintendent |
| Fire Inspector | Fish and Game Warden | Security Guard |

### ENGINEERING [05.01]

| | | |
|---|---|---|
| Air Analyst | Land Surveyor | Tool Designer |
| Aeronautical Engineer | Civil Engineer | Mechanical Engineer |
| Agricultural Engineer | Electronics Technician | Software Technician |

### MANAGERIAL WORK: MECHANICAL [05.02]

| | | |
|---|---|---|
| Food Processing Plant Manager | Electric Power Superintendent | Waste Control Supervisor |
| Radio/TV Technical Director | | |

## ENGINEERING TECHNOLOGY [05.03]

| | | |
|---|---|---|
| Air-Traffic Controller | Mechanical Drafter | Test Technician |
| Building Inspector | Technical Illustrator | Material Scheduler |
| Pollution-Control Technician | Safety Inspector | |
| Marine Surveyor | | |

## AIR AND WATER VEHICLE OPERATION [05.04]

| | | |
|---|---|---|
| Airplane Pilot | Ferryboat Captain | Fishing Vessel Captain |
| Riverboat Master | Tugboat Mate | |
| Flying Instructor | | |

## CRAFT TECHNOLOGY [05.05]

| | | |
|---|---|---|
| Bricklayer | Electrician | Refrigeration Mechanic |
| Carpenter | Automobile Body Repairer | Diesel Mechanic |
| Furnace Installer-Repairer | Machinist | Optician |
| Paperhanger | Welder | Dental Laboratory Manager |
| Plumber | Tool-and-Die Maker | Job Printer |
| Avionics Technician | Aircraft Mechanic | Chef |
| Cable TV Technician | Automobile Mechanic | Furniture Upholsterer |

## SYSTEMS OPERATION [05.06]

| | | |
|---|---|---|
| Boiler Operator | Gas-Pumping Station Operator | Waste Water Treatment Plant Operator |
| Ship Engineer | | |
| Electric Power Plant Operator | | |

## QUALITY CONTROL [05.07, 06.03]

| | | |
|---|---|---|
| Airplane Inspector | Meat Grader | Quality-Control Inspector |
| Garment Inspector | Cheese Grader | |
| Machine Tester | | |

## LAND VEHICLE OPERATION [05.08, 09.03]

| | | |
|---|---|---|
| Ambulance Driver | Locomotive Engineer | Chauffeur |
| Bus Driver | Truck Driver | Driving Instructor |

## MATERIAL CONTROL [05.09]

| | | |
|---|---|---|
| Shipping and Receiving Clerk | Cargo Agent | Laboratory Clerk |

## CRAFTS [05.10]

| | | |
|---|---|---|
| Appliance Repairer | Cook | TV-Radio Repairer |
| Baker | Farm Equipment Mechanic | Diver |
| Painter | Roofer | |

## EQUIPMENT OPERATION [05.11]

| | | |
|---|---|---|
| Bulldozer Operator | Crane Operator | Tractor Operator |
| Power-Shovel Operator | Machine Driller | Asphalt Paving Supervisor |

## PRODUCTION TECHNOLOGY AND PRODUCTION WORK [06.01, 06.02]

| | | |
|---|---|---|
| Weaver | Instrument Mechanic | Production Supervisor |
| Dry Cleaner | Electronics Inspector | Punch-Press Operator |
| Feed Mill Supervisor | Machine Setter | Assembler |

## CRAFT ARTS [01.06]

| | | |
|---|---|---|
| Engraver | Jeweler | Taxidermist |
| Model Maker | Sign Painter | Graphic Arts Technician |

## INVESTIGATIVE

## PHYSICAL SCIENCES [02.01]

| | | |
|---|---|---|
| Astronomer | Geographer | Meteorologist |
| Chemist | Geologist | Seismologist |
| Environmental Analyst | Mathematician | Physical Science Teacher |

## LIFE SCIENCES [02.02]

| | | |
|---|---|---|
| Animal Scientist | Food Chemist | Plant Pathologist |
| Biologist | Food Technologist | Soil Conservationist |
| Coroner | Plant Breeder | Life Science Teacher |

## MEDICAL SCIENCES [02.03]

| | | |
|---|---|---|
| Anesthesiologist | Internist | Pediatrician |
| Cardiologist | Optometrist | Surgeon |
| Dentist | General Physician | Veterinarian |

## LABORATORY TECHNOLOGY [02.04]

| | | |
|---|---|---|
| Dietetic Technician | Animal Health Technician | Food Tester |
| Laboratory Technician | Embalmer | Pharmacist |

## MATHEMATICS AND STATISTICS [11.01]

| | | |
|---|---|---|
| Actuary | Information Scientist | Statistician |
| Computer Programmer | Financial Analyst | Systems Analyst |

## SOCIAL RESEARCH [11.03]

| | | |
|---|---|---|
| Archeologist | Urban Planner | Archivist |
| Historian | Industrial Psychologist | Occupational Analyst |
| Developmental Psychologist | Economist | Sociologist |

## ARTISTIC

## LITERARY ARTS [01.01]

| | | |
|---|---|---|
| Biographer | Critic | Playwright |
| Book Editor | Editorial Writer | Poet |
| Copy Writer | Film Editor | Writer |

## VISUAL ARTS [01.02]

| | | |
|---|---|---|
| Architect | Commercial Designer | Landscape Architect |
| Art Appraiser | Graphic Designer | Photographer |
| Art Teacher | Illustrator | Sculptor |
| Clothes Designer | Interior Designer | Set Designer |

## DRAMA AND DANCE [01.03, 01.05, 01.07, 01.08]

| | | |
|---|---|---|
| Actor/Actress | Dancer | Disk Jockey |
| Choreographer | Model | Director |
| Comedian | Dance or Drama Teacher | Radio and TV Announcer |

## MUSIC [01.04]

| | | |
|---|---|---|
| Choral Director | Musician | Singer |
| Composer | Orchestra Conductor | Music Director |
| Music Teacher | Orchestrator | Arranger |

# SOCIAL

## SOCIAL SERVICES [10.01]

| | | |
|---|---|---|
| School Counselor | Parole Officer | Clinical Psychologist |
| Dean of Students | School Psychologist | Vocational-Rehabilitation Counselor |
| Clergy or Religious Worker | Social Worker | |

## NURSING, THERAPY, AND SPECIALIZED TRAINING [10.02]

| | | |
|---|---|---|
| Athletic Trainer | Nurse | Respiratory Therapist |
| Dental Hygienist | Radiologic (X-ray) Technician | Teacher for the Disabled |
| Nurse Instructor | | Kindergarten Teacher |
| Occupational Therapist | | |

## CHILD AND ADULT CARE [10.03]

| | | |
|---|---|---|
| Emergency Medical Technician | Audiometrist | Practical Nurse |

## EDUCATIONAL AND LIBRARY SERVICES [11.02]

| | | |
|---|---|---|
| Librarian | High School Teacher | Vocational Training Teacher |
| Elementary Teacher | Home Economist | County Agricultural Agent |

## SPORTS [12.01, 12.02]

| | | |
|---|---|---|
| Head Coach | Umpire | Rodeo Performer |
| Professional Athlete | Acrobat | Sports Instructor |

## ENTERPRISING

## SALES [08.01, 08.02]

| | | |
|---|---|---|
| Auctioneer | Insurance Sales Agent | Travel Agent |
| Buyer | Real Estate Sales Agent | Computer Sales Representative |
| Fund Raiser | Auto Salesperson | |
| Pawn Broker | | |

## HOSPITALITY, BEAUTY, AND CUSTOMER SERVICES [09.01, 09.02, 09.04]

| | | |
|---|---|---|
| Barber | Cosmetologist | Recreation Leader |
| Bartender | Flight Attendant | Automobile Rental Clerk |

## LAW [11.04]

| | | |
|---|---|---|
| Arbitrator | Hearing Officer | Lawyer |
| District Attorney | Judge | Paralegal Assistant |

## BUSINESS ADMINISTRATION [11.05]

| | | |
|---|---|---|
| City Manager | Purchasing Agent | College Business Manager |
| Office Manager | Bank President | Public Works Commissioner |

## FINANCE [11.06]

| | | |
|---|---|---|
| Accountant | Treasurer | Securities Trader |
| Appraiser | Loan Officer | Market Research Analyst |

## SERVICES ADMINISTRATION [11.07]

| | | |
|---|---|---|
| School Principal | College President | Welfare Director |
| Hospital Administrator | Curator | Public Health Educator |

## COMMUNICATIONS [11.08]

| | | |
|---|---|---|
| Newspaper Editor | Reporter | Translator |
| News Director | Newscaster | Technical Writer |

## PROMOTION [11.09]

| | | |
|---|---|---|
| Fundraising Director | Advertising Manager | Public Relations |
| Lobbyist | Promotion Manager | Representative |
| Foreign Service Officer | | |

## REGULATIONS ENFORCEMENT [11.10]

| | | |
|---|---|---|
| Bank Examiner | Immigration Inspector | Safety Inspector |
| Customs Inspector | Industrial Hygienist | Fraud Investigator |

## BUSINESS MANAGEMENT [11.11]

| | | |
|---|---|---|
| Camp Director | Hotel or Motel Manager | Health Club Manager |
| Property Manager | Retail Store Manager | Apartment House Manager |

## CONTRACTS AND CLAIMS [11.12]

| | | |
|---|---|---|
| Booking Manager | Claim Examiner | Literary Agent |
| Claim Adjuster | Lease Buyer | Real Estate Agent |

## CONVENTIONAL

### ADMINISTRATIVE DETAIL [07.01]

| Town Clerk | Driver's License Examiner | Title Examiner |
| Medical Secretary | Secretary | Credit Analyst |

### MATHEMATICAL AND FINANCIAL DETAIL [07.02, 07.03]

| Payroll Clerk | Insurance Claim Examiner | Bank Teller |
| Tax Clerk | Post Office Clerk | Account Analyst |

### ORAL COMMUNICATIONS [07.04]

| Information Clerk | Airline Reservation Agent | Loan Interviewer |
| Telephone Operator | Hotel or Motel Clerk | Dispatcher |

### RECORDS PROCESSING [07.05, 07.06, 07.07]

| General Clerk | Mail Room Supervisor | Title Searcher |
| Mail Carrier | Stenographer | Billing Machine Operator |
| Computer Operator | Medical Record Technician | Fingerprint Clerk |

### LEARNING MORE

I'm sure you will want to learn more about the occupations you identified. You will want answers to these questions: What does a person do in "X" occupation? Would I like it? What kind of training is required? Which Special Skills do I need to learn? These are all good questions.

An easy way to begin answering questions like these is to turn to an excellent book called the *Guide for Occupational Exploration,* or the *GOE.* A newer version is called *The Complete Guide for Occupational Exploration.* Your school or public library should have one or the other version. The *GOE* is organized according to four-digit numbers. These numbers start with 01.01 and end with 12.02. You can see these numbers in brackets (e.g., [01.01]) next to the groups of occupations on the preceding pages.

You can use these four-digit numbers to find information in the *GOE.* It's easy, and it's surprising what you can learn from this book. To see what I mean, look at the next two illustrations. They show part of the 01.01 section of the *GOE.*

*01.01*

## SPECIALIZED TRAINING FOR SUBGROUPS

| JOBS | EDUCATION/TRAINING | WHERE OBTAINED |
|------|-------------------|----------------|
| **01.01.01 EDITING** | | |
| All in Editing | Experience | Related jobs within the same industry |
| Editor, Film (motion pic.; radio & tv broad.) | Cinematography, TV Operations, Film Editing, Audio-Visual Techniques | Military (Navy, Air Force, Marine Corps, Coast Guard), Apprenticeship, Two-Year College, University |
| Producer (motion pic.) | Motion Picture Production, Cinematography, Drama, Stagecraft, Technical Theatre | School for Performing Arts, Repertory Theatre, Drama School, Two-Year College, University |
| | Marketing, Advertising | University, Business School |
| Reader (motion pic.; radio & tv broad.) | Broadcast Journalism, Writing (Prose and Technical) | Two-Year College, University |
| Editor, Book (print. & pub.) | Literary Genre, Writing (Prose and Technical), Editing and Production | University (English or Communications Department) |
| Editor, Greeting Card (print. & pub.) | Marketing, Management | University, Two-Year College, Business School |
| **01.01.02 CREATIVE WRITING** | | |
| All in Creative Writing | Practice, Competition, Publication | College, University, Community Theatre, Local Publications |
| Screen Writer (motion pic.; radio & tv broad.) | Writing (Screen, Play, Prose, Short Story), Cinematography | Military (All branches), School for Performing Arts, Repertory Theatre, Two-Year College, University |
| Librettist, Lyricist (profess. & kin.) | Music Theory | Music Conservatory, Two-Year College |
| Playwright, Poet, Writer (profess. & kin.) | Writing (Screen, Play, Prose, Poetry, Short Story, Fiction, Non-Fiction) | High School, School for Performing Arts, Two-Year College, University |
| Editorial Writer (print. & pub.), Biographer (profess. & kin.) | Research Methodology, Prose Writing | University |
| Copy Writer (profess. & kin.) | Prose Writing, Copy Writing, Advertising | High School, Two-Year College, University |
| Continuity Writer (radio & tv) | Copy Writing, News Writing, Radio and TV Operations | Two-Year College, University |
| **01.01.03 CRITIQUING** | | |
| Critic (print. & pub.; radio & tv broad.) | Job experience, Special knowledge[1] | On the job, High School, Two-Year College, University |
| | Writing (Prose, Technical) | High School, Two-Year College, University |

1  Critics may specialize in art, music, drama, literature, economics, science, etc.

■ **Organizations and Agencies to Contact for Additional Information about Literary Arts Jobs:**
- Allied Business Writers of America
- American Association of Advertising Agencies
- American Cinema Editors
- American Guild of Authors and Composers
- American Theater Critics Association
- Associated Writing Programs
- International Association of Independent Producers
- International Creative Writers' League
- National Association of Editorial Writers
- National Association of Science Writers
- National Conference of Editorial Writers
- National Writers' Club
- Outdoor Writers' Association of America
- Society of American Travel Writers

97

## 01.01
## Literary Arts

| GOE/CGOE# & SUBGROUP DOT TITLE AND INDUSTRY | DOT CODE | STR. FAC. | TRAINING* R-M-L-SVP | GOE/CGOE# & SUBGROUP DOT TITLE AND INDUSTRY | DOT CODE | STR. FAC. | TRAINING* R-M-L-SVP |
|---|---|---|---|---|---|---|---|
| **01.01.01 EDITING** | | | | EDITORIAL WRITER (print. & pub.) | 131.067-022 | S | 5-3-5-8 |
| PRODUCER (motion picture) | 187.167-174 | S | 6-5-6-8 | CROSSWORD-PUZZLE MAKER (print. & pub.) | 139.087-010 | S | 5-2-5-6 |
| READER (motion picture; radio-tv broad.) | 131.087-014 | S | 5-2-5-6 | BIOGRAPHER (profess. & kin.) | 052.067-010 | S | 5-2-5-7 |
| STORY EDITOR (motion picture; radio-tv broad.) | 132.037-026 | S | 6-2-6-8 | COPY WRITER (profess. & kin.) | 131.067-014 | S | 5-2-5-7 |
| SUPERVISING FILM-OR-VIDEOTAPE EDITOR (motion picture; radio-tv broad.) | 962.132-010 | M | 5-3-5-8 | HUMORIST (profess. & kin.) | 131.067-026 | S | 6-2-6-8 |
| | | | | LIBRETTIST (profess. & kin.) | 131.067-030 | S | 6-2-6-7 |
| FILM OR VIDEOTAPE EDITOR (motion picture; radio-tv broad.) | 962.262-010 | L | 5-2-4-8 | LYRICIST (profess. & kin.) | 131.067-034 | S | 6-2-6-7 |
| | | | | PLAYWRIGHT (profess. & kin.) | 131.067-038 | S | 6-2-6-8 |
| EDITOR, PUBLICATIONS (print. & pub.) | 132.037-022 | S | 6-3-6-8 | POET (profess. & kin.) | 131.067-042 | S | 6-2-6-7 |
| EDITOR, BOOK (print. & pub.) | 132.067-014 | S | 6-3-6-8 | WRITER, PROSE, FICTION AND NONFICTION (profess. & kin.) | 131.067-046 | S | 6-3-6-8 |
| EDITOR, GREETING CARD (print. & pub.) | 132.067-022 | S | 5-2-5-6 | CONTINUITY WRITER (radio-tv broad.) | 131.087-010 | S | 5-2-5-7 |
| CONTINUITY DIRECTOR (radio-tv broad.) | 132.037-010 | S | 5-2-5-8 | | | | |
| | | | | **01.01.03 CRITIQUING** | | | |
| **01.01.02 CREATIVE WRITING** | | | | CRITIC (print. & pub.; radio-tv broad.) | 131.067-018 | S | 6-2-6-8 |
| SCREEN WRITER (motion picture; radio-tv broad.) | 131.067-050 | S | 6-2-6-7 | | | | |

*See tables in Chapter One for explanation of strength factor and training codes.

The *GOE* also gives the Special Skills needed for the occupations listed. For example, the occupations in the 01.01, Literary Arts, section require the following skills:

\_\_\_ Influence the opinion of people through words.

\_\_\_ Understand and apply rules of grammar and have a large vocabulary.

\_\_\_ Edit and interpret the written work of others.

\_\_\_ Create written works such as stories, plays, or poetry.

\_\_\_ Produce art forms like screen plays, films, radio or TV programs that express original ideas, attract attention, or influence opinions.

As you can see, you can learn a lot from the *GOE!*

Many other handbooks can help you find information on the occupations that appeal to you. In addition to the *GOE*, I recommend the *Occupational Outlook Handbook* and the *Encyclopedia of Careers and Vocational Guidance.* Your school and public libraries will have these.

In addition to books, there are many other interesting and helpful ways to learn about skills and occupations. Good examples are computerized guidance systems, interviews with people in the work you are considering, and volunteer work. These learning options are described at the end of Chapter 10.

PART two

# THE FOUNDATION SKILLS

# The Basic Skills

**Y**es, you have been studying basic skills like reading and mathematics for years, but do you know how these skills are used on a job? *Often workers use these skills in different ways than students do.* In this chapter, you will learn which reading, writing, math, listening, and speaking skills are important in the workplace and how workers use them.

You will *also* learn how to strengthen these skills. I searched for the best teachers I could find and invited them to write learning activities for you. They did a superb job! These activities are great and I know you will enjoy doing them. Plus, they will strengthen your skills, make you more powerful, and prepare you for the opportunities ahead.

## READING SKILLS

You need strong reading skills. All jobs require them. Workers today spend an average of two hours a day reading such things as letters, records, tables, charts, directories, manuals, and computer terminals. They read to get the information they need to do their work. You will need to read for details, and to do it rapidly and accurately.

Workers need to

1. identify the relevant details, facts, and specifications in what they are reading.

2. locate information, for example, in books and manuals, from graphs and schedules.

3. find the meaning of unknown or technical words and phrases.

4. judge the accuracy of reports.

5. use computers to find information.

I think you can already see how the reading skills needed at work are somewhat different from the reading skills you use in school work. You will see this difference more clearly as we look at the other basic skills in this chapter.

### "Workers"

I use this word frequently. Please keep in mind that it includes all people who work for pay. A doctor in Kansas, the head of Ford Motor Company in Detroit, a trumpet player with the San Francisco Symphony Orchestra, a bus driver in Boston, or a small business owner in Texas—these are all workers.

To give you a clearer picture of the reading skills needed at work, I have chosen two occupations to illustrate these skills.

**SHIPPING AND RECEIVING CLERK.** *At Exide Electronics, Leon Newkirk has the important job of keeping track of the materials that come into the plant. Whether it's wire, bolts, rolls of copper, or light bulbs that come through the plant door, it's his job to make a record of the item in the computer system. In this way, anyone in the plant can check into the computer system to be sure that all the parts needed to make the electric power systems (see my interview with Al Williams, p. 9, for more on this product) are on hand.*

**Leon Newkirk concentrates on correctly entering information from the packing slip into the computer system.**

Leon explains how he does his job.

When the trucks come up to the back door, we unload them, and open up the boxes. I take out the packing slip and count the parts to make sure that what the slip said is in the box is what we got. Then I bring the slip over to my desk and key it into the computer. The computer prints out a receipt that has three copies. The gold copy goes to the receiving department; the green and white copies go into the box with the parts. Then the QC [quality control person] comes by and checks the parts to see if they are OK, stamps the receipts, and takes the green copy. The white copy stays in the box with the parts, which go to the stockroom.

As you can see from this example, Leon needs excellent reading skills. As he reads, he needs to find the important details and check the accuracy of the packing slip and other papers, as well as the information he sees on the computer screen.

Leon is also a good example of a person using all the Foundation Skills. For example, he is part of a team effort. The rest of the team, everyone at Exide, is depending on him to do a fast and accurate job. In addition to teamwork, Leon has the responsibility skills needed. He has to concentrate on what he is doing. There are a lot of details to his job, and he has to pay careful attention even though the task may be boring at times. The whole plant depends upon him. If he enters the wrong numbers into the computer, the mistake could result in a delay costing the company thousands of dollars.

**SWITCHBOARD OPERATOR-RECEPTIONIST.** *Delores Cole works for a large bank. Hundreds of people call each day needing information, and Delores is the first person they talk to. Delores must be able to direct each person's call to the department or person who can answer the question. She uses her skills in reading to quickly and accurately find that information. For example, in the photo below she is looking in the bank's phone directory for the right telephone number.*

**Delores Cole reads the bank's telephone directory to find whom to direct the caller to.**

## Activities to Develop Your Reading Skills by Patsy Douville

Being able to analyze information will be essential in the future; you need to strengthen that skill *now*.

**1.** Follow an important news story, in which you are especially interested, in both the newspaper and on television. Analyze the main issues or ideas of the story as they are covered on the television news. Now read about the same story in the newspaper. Do both the television and newspaper report the same facts of the story? Does one format appear to be more or less objective than the other? In other words, do you feel that either the TV news or the newspaper is trying to influence your thinking in some way, or are only the important facts being reported? Write down your ideas so that you can analyze them further as you follow the news story over a period of time.

**2.** Stores and businesses use advertisements as a way to convince customers to buy their products or use their services. It is especially important that you analyze advertisements to make certain you're getting the best deal for your money. Find the section of the newspaper in which grocery stores list their sales. Which stores offer the best bargains on the same items, such as soft drinks or snack foods? How much cheaper are the "sale" prices than the regular prices? Why do you think stores put particular items on sale during certain times of the week, such as just before the start of the weekend?

*Being able to read ideas and picture them in the mind is called mental imagery. This skill is an effective tool for organizing information and solving problems. You can improve your mental imagery skills with these activities.*

**3.** Draw on paper the images or pictures that your mind creates. For example, the next time you read a story try drawing a picture of the characters or settings that the author describes. As you read, change or add to the picture depending upon how your mental images change as the story progresses. If a friend is reading the same story, compare your pictures to see how alike or different they are.

**4.** Using the real estate section of the newspaper, carefully read the description of a house that interests you. Based on the information provided in the ad, construct a mental image of this house. What details of your image were left to your imagination because they weren't included in the ad? How important are these details and why do you think they were left out of the ad? Did the ad give you enough information upon which to make an *informed* decision about purchasing the house? Now draw on paper a picture of your house "image." How closely does it match the description in the ad? Did you add or leave out important details?

*Good readers often read for the purpose of locating specific information. The next activity will strengthen this skill.*

**5.** Using either *TV Guide* or the television section of the newspaper, find the night of the week on which the greatest number of comedy shows are presented

between the hours of 7:00 p.m. and 11:00 p.m. Find the day of the week on which the most hour-long drama shows are presented between the hours of 7:00 p.m. and 11:00 p.m. On what television channel, and on what day of the week, would you be most likely to see shows about nature/animals between the hours of 10:00 a.m. and 5:00 p.m.? On what television channel, and on what day of the week, would you be able to watch the most sports shows between the hours of 10:00 a.m. and 5:00 p.m.?

**6.** Using the telephone book, find the number of Chinese restaurants in your city/town. Find the name, telephone number, and address of a doctor who could fit you with contact lenses. Find the telephone number of the business, nearest to where you live, at which you could have your car repainted. Find the address of a pet store at which you could buy tropical fish. How many people are listed in the telephone book with your last name?

**7.** Find the section of the newspaper in which you could locate weather information. What are today's predicted high/low temperatures for your city/town? At what times, for this date, will the sun rise and set? Which United States cities had the highest and lowest recorded temperatures for the day?

*One effective tool for finding the meaning of unknown words is to continue reading the rest of the sentence or paragraph in which the sentence is located in order to see whether you can make a "smart guess" about what a word means. This next activity will give you practice in doing this.*

**8.** With a group of friends, select a magazine article or book about something that interests you. Read carefully, paying particular attention to unfamiliar words. From words around them, try to figure out unknown word meanings. If you need to check your answer, look the word up in the dictionary *after* you've tried using context clues. However, you'll sometimes find that you won't need to waste time going to the dictionary because you will often be able to define unknown words just by *reading* for meaning.

**Patsy Douville** has been a teacher for many years. She has taught in a number of states in the U.S. and spent four years teaching in Japan. She has been named "Teacher of the Year" and "Outstanding Educator of the Month," and was selected as one of the "Twenty Most Outstanding Teaching Assistants" at North Carolina State University. Patsy has always been interested in helping students become better readers and appreciate the joy of reading. Recently, she worked with over 300 students in order to learn how imagery, or mental pictures, affect reading and learning. Patsy believes that good readers use many learning "tools" to help them understand and enjoy what they read.

## WRITING SKILLS

You will need strong writing skills. In your work, you will want to describe what you observe, state your opinions, and ask questions. You will request, explain, illustrate, and convince. It is important that you do these things clearly, rapidly, completely, and accurately, both on paper and with a computer. Below are five writing skills needed by all workers:

1. Communicate thoughts, ideas, information, and messages in writing.

2. Record information completely and accurately.

3. Create documents, including letters, manuals, reports, and graphs.

4. Check, edit, and revise documents for correct information, appropriate emphasis, grammar, spelling, and punctuation.

5. Use computers to communicate information.

Here is one example of how writing skills are used in all jobs.

**PERSONNEL REPRESENTATIVE.** *Andrea Carroll conducts all the new employee orientations and keeps a record of every applicant to each position, whether they are hired or not. She also helps her boss on writing projects and handling correspondence. All these jobs require strong writing skills.*

**Andrea Carroll needs strong writing skills in her job.**

LJ: Tell me about the writing skills you need in your job.

Andrea: When you start out in this type of position you don't do much writing on your own, but it increases as you gain experience. I now do a lot of writing on my own.

LJ: How important are things like grammar, punctuation, spelling?

Andrea: They are important from day one. A good foundation in grammar is vital. For spelling, you can at least use a dictionary or the spell check built into most word processing packages. So if you are not a good speller you can still do this job. But grammar, sentence structure, and punctuation you must know; you will need knowledge of them all the time.

LJ:     What skill or skills do you think are particularly useful in your job?

Andrea: I need good keyboarding skills. I think you need this skill in most any job today in the business world. Even the managers need that now, because they do a lot of input themselves. Keyboarding is one of the essentials. I would think writing skills and punctuation would be the second most important.

Here are two more examples of how writing skills are used.

**LAW ENFORCEMENT OFFICER.** *The officer writes reports of accidents and crimes to put into computers, talks to witnesses, summarizes the information, and writes it down in the order it happened. The officer then proofreads the report, makes corrections, and turns it in.*

**LICENSED PRACTICAL NURSE.** *The LPN records the patient's activity and other observations on a variety of forms, observing and recording the patient's body temperature, blood pressure, alertness, and other characteristics. The nurse writes down changes in medication and other vital information.*

## Activities to Develop Your Writing Skills by Dawn Woody

**1.** After looking at a map of the United States with your friends, choose a place you've never been and write specific directions on how to get there from your hometown. Be sure to use highway and interstate numbers as well as towns and cities you would go through to reach your destination. When possible, estimate mileage and use directional indicators (i.e., north, south, northwest, etc.). Exchange your written directions to see how easy they are to follow.

**2.** Learn the format for business and personal letters. Write a letter to the chamber of commerce in the place you'd like to visit. Ask for information about the location (e.g., historical locations, recreational facilities, sporting events, etc.).

**3.** Play a game of "I Spy" with a group of friends. Write a paragraph with three clues describing an object or person in the room. Try to include specific details, and be creative in the wording of your clues. For example, if you are describing a clock, you might say that "it has hands that are never still." Read your paragraph aloud and have others guess your topic.

**4.** Examine the front page of your local newspaper. Using it as an example, create your own newspaper front page based on an important day or event such as a birthday, holiday, family vacation, or even summer camp. Write an appropriate and catchy headline for each story and be sure to include either photographs or drawings with captions to compliment your stories.

**5.** Draw names among a group of friends or family members. Observe that person for a day, taking notes of specific mannerisms and/or habits. Write a character sketch of your person. Be sure to include details from your notes instead of simply describing how the person looks. Share your sketch with others in the group to see if the person being described recognizes himself/herself.

**6.** Imagine that you have unlimited funds to spend during one 24-hour period. Write a realistic, detailed agenda of how you would spend your day.

**7.** With a friend, write a summary of a favorite television show, movie, or book. Include 5-10 deliberate, although not necessarily obvious, mistakes. Include spelling, capitalization, and punctuation, as well as grammar, in your mistakes. Trade papers and try to correct the mistakes.

**8.** Start a brag book of things at which you are particularly good. Write out detailed directions as well as a materials list for each activity and date it. For example, if you can maintain a beautiful lawn or build a delicious club sandwich, start out by listing all the equipment and/or supplies you use and then write a chronological description of what you do (e.g., 1. I fill the mower with gas, or 1. I arrange four slices of bread in the toaster). Before long you will find that you are talented at many things!

**Dawn Woody** is a former middle and high school language arts and English teacher. After teaching eight years in grades 7-11, Dawn returned to school and received her master's in English education. She was selected as a fellow with the nationally known Capital Area Writing Project, where she studied the best use of writing in the classroom. Dawn currently supervises secondary student teachers of English at North Carolina State University. She is also a reviewer for Media Evaluation and Technology Services at the North Carolina Department of Public Instruction. As you can see from the above activities, her skills in teaching writing are highly valued.

## Word Processing

Do you know how to write using a computer? This is called word processing. If you know how to use a computer in this way, be sure to do some of the writing activities described above using a computer. If you haven't learned the skill of word processing, you will want to. It is a skill everyone needs to learn. It's fun and not difficult to learn. You will really enjoy writing this way, and it is a skill you will use often in the years ahead. You will use it to write school reports, at your place of work, and in your personal life. To learn more about word processing, talk with your school library media specialist or English teacher.

## MATHEMATICS SKILLS

Today's worker needs math skills. The work of a travel agent is a good example of this need. The agent may need to plan a customer's vacation trip so that it costs no more than a certain amount of money. To do this, the agent

- Finds out how much the customer can spend on the vacation and the types of things he or she wants to do.

- Calls places to find out what the transportation and housing costs are.

- Enters these figures in a computer and calculates the total cost of the trip and the agent's commission.

- Makes changes if needed so that the total cost fits the budgeted amount.

- Prepares a bill for the customer, and gives the customer a receipt when the bill is paid.

The work of a travel agent is just one example of how math skills are used. You will need the following math skills for your job:

1. Use numbers, fractions, and percentages to solve practical problems.

2. Make reasonable estimates of arithmetic results without a calculator.

3. Use tables, graphs, diagrams, and charts to obtain numerical information.

4. Use computers to enter, retrieve, and change numerical data.

5. Use computers to communicate data, choosing the best form (e.g., line or bar graph, tables, pie charts) to present data.

Below are two more occupations that illustrate how math is used.

**MANAGER OF TRAINING SERVICES.** *James Amos is in charge of all printing for his corporation. Math skills are important in his job.*

LJ: How is math used in printing?

James: Cutting paper is a good example, especially when you use large sheet sizes. Often when you order paper, it doesn't come precut and you need to use a larger size. When I tell an employee that I need 500 8 1/2" x 11" sheets cut out of paper measuring 35 1/2" x 25 1/2", that employee needs to be able to take that larger sheet, diagram it, and see how many sheets can be cut out of it. I need to determine how many large sheets will be required to get the 500 sheets of 8 1/2" x 11".

LJ: How else do you use math skills? Do you do anything in the way of cost estimating?

James: Yes. When we have a job, we need to put a price on it. We need to understand the amount of labor required, the amount of paper used, and how much the paper costs. We need to be able to calculate figures. We do a lot of that.

LJ: You have a great variety of skills? Skills in math, graphic design, computers, and managing others. How did you learn them?

James: Most of my skills have been learned through my organization, PICA [Printing Industries of the Carolinas Association]. Their workshops have helped me a lot, because when I first started out I was running a printing press by trial and error. I started going to a lot of classes, and I took a lot of computer classes to understand the computer system graphics. But many things I learned through putting in a lot of late hours.

LJ: When you say you spent "a lot of late hours," what do you mean?

James: If you plan on succeeding in anything that you do, 8 to 5, or working 40 hours a week, is not always enough. When it all gets quiet [and other workers have left] and you need to focus on something that needs to get done, you just have to take more time and work late hours after everyone else has gone home. You have got to go that extra mile in order to obtain quality along with quantity in anything you do.

**DENTIST.** *Bettie McKaig has many skills as a dentist; math is among them. She uses math in many ways. One of the ways unique to dentistry is to measure the depth of the space between a tooth and the gum that surrounds it. She slides what is called a periodontal probe down between the tooth and the gum, and measures the depth. This measurement, explains Bettie, "helps us determine the health of the gum tissue. A measurement of three to four millimeters is considered healthy. Anything beyond that you have a concern." The measurement is then marked on a chart. "We take six measurements per tooth for the periodontal charting." In the photo below you can see the probe in Dr. McKaig's right hand.*

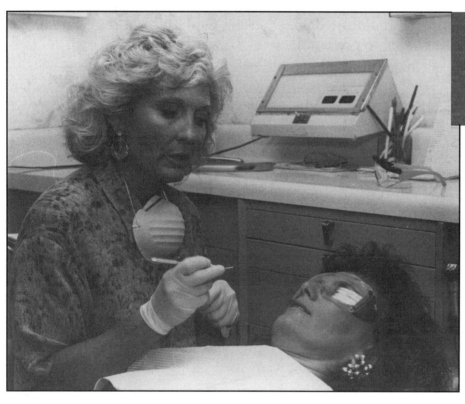

**Dr. McKaig's measurements must be precise. She works in tenths of millimeters every day.**

## Activities to Develop Your Math Skills by Cleo Meek

*The first activity will improve your ability to use whole and decimal numbers, fractions, and percentages to solve practical problems.*

**1.** Many of your friends will want to buy a car as soon as they are old enough. Ask several of them to write the name and the cost of the car they would like to own. Then ask them to go to a bank, credit union, finance company, or car dealership and find out how much the monthly payments would be on this car if paid off in two years, three years, four years, and five years. Have each of them compute the total amount they would have to pay to finance the car for each of these times. Compare how much more expensive it is to pay for a car over a five-year period than it is to pay for a car over a two-year period. Ask them which source of financing was the least expensive and which was the most expensive. Use the information you have gained in this activity whenever you have to pay for something over a period of time.

*It's interesting to learn how mathematics is used on different jobs. Try out this next activity with some friends.*

**2.** Ask several of your friends to work with you on an investigation. During the next week each of you will need to make note of the times you see someone using mathematics on his or her job, along with the ways they are using mathematics. At the end of the week, put all this information in a list or chart. Indicate if more than one person used mathematics the same way. Get these same friends to help you ask several people who are working how they use mathematics on their jobs. Make a list of your findings and compare it with the earlier list you and your friends compiled. This activity should enable you and your friends to see some of the interesting ways mathematics is used on the job.

*In your future work you will need to obtain and communicate numerical information. This next activity will give you practice in doing this.*

**3.** Ask some of your friends to find all the graphs and charts they can in magazines, newspapers, or books for a one-week period. Work with your friends to organize these graphs and charts by type, e.g., line, bar, circle, table, chart. Determine which ones are the easiest to read and understand. Determine which ones are the most difficult to read and understand. Determine which ones are misleading. Use the knowledge you have gained in this activity the next time you have to use tables, graphs, diagrams, and charts to display or interpret numerical data.

*In your future work you will use a computer to communicate data. This next activity displays one way to do this.*

**4.** The fastest animal is the cheetah, which can travel at 70 mph; the slowest animal is the garden snail, which can only travel at 0.03 mph. Get two of your friends to work with you so that each of you will find the speeds of six other animals. You can get information on animal speeds from reference books like the annual *Information Please Almanac.* If you know how to use a computer, display this information in a table and in a graph. If not, get someone to show you how to use the computer to do this. This activity should enable you to use a computer to arrange data in a table and to make a graph of the data.

*The next activity offers one way to use a computer to enter, retrieve, and change numerical data.*

**5.** Imagine some students decide to start a summer business doing odd jobs for people in their neighborhood. They ask you to be their business manager to maintain records of the business's financial dealings. One of the members of the business says the job would be easier if you would use a computer with a spreadsheet program. Learn all you can about a spreadsheet, and when and how to use one. Some of the most common ones used are AppleWorks, Lotus, ClarisWorks, Microsoft Works, and First Choice. Explain what you learned to a friend or members of your class. Explain to them how a spreadsheet can be used

to keep a business's financial records. This activity should help you learn how to use a computer spreadsheet and where it can best be used.

*You will enjoy the following long-range project.*

**6.** Get several groups of four students each to work together for a six-month period of time to determine which group can "earn the most money." Each group is to assume that they have $100,000 to invest in three different stocks listed on the stock exchange. They have one week to make their choices. Once they have chosen their stocks, they are to make a graph to show the weekly progress of their stocks. At the end of the six-month period, each group is to report to the class on the performance of their stocks. The report should include such topics as why they chose their stocks; how much each stock earned or lost; what was the highest and lowest listing for their stocks; and whether they think their stocks are good choices for future investment. Have all the members of your class determine the "best investment group." Use the information you have learned about the stock market in this activity to explain the stock listings in the newspaper to a relative or a friend not in your class.

**Dr. Cleo Meek** is a mathematics consultant who works with mathematics teachers to help them become better teachers. His aim is to help mathematics teachers make mathematics interesting to students, and for students to realize that mathematics is worthwhile for them to learn. Before becoming a mathematics consultant, Dr. Meek was a mathematics teacher in Oklahoma and Arizona. He received academic scholarships to attend the University of North Carolina at Chapel Hill and Duke University. If you study hard, enjoy mathematics, and make good grades, you may be able to get a scholarship to go on to college.

## SPEAKING SKILLS

You will speak with many people each day at work. In talking with co-workers or customers, you may explain how something works, or describe procedures to be followed. You may ask questions to identify why something is not working, or speak in a way that will encourage co-workers to express themselves fully. It is important to do this clearly and effectively. Below are the skills needed.

1. Organize ideas and communicate oral messages appropriate to listener and situations.

2. Select appropriate language, tone of voice, gestures, and level of complexity appropriate to audience and occasion.

3. Speak clearly; ask questions when needed.

**CHILD CARE CENTER DIRECTOR.** *Rebecca Bowman, the director of the Campus Child Care Center, is a good example of someone who uses speaking skills. In the photo below, she is talking with William Hartzell and his son, Steven, who is a student at the Center.*

Rebecca Bowman, the child care center director, speaks with a parent and his son.

In addition to being skilled in speaking with parents and their children, Rebecca needs to be able to speak well to her teachers, the Center's board of directors, and people at public meetings. Rebecca made this comment about speaking to her teachers: "It is a difficult thing to do if you are not used to it—trying to let them know what they need to do or must do, whatever you are telling them, without stepping on toes. You don't need a communications degree, but you do need good speaking skills." For more on Rebecca's job, see Chapter 8 (p. 103).

**DENTAL HYGIENIST.** *Cynthia Wilson, a registered dental hygienist, uses her speaking skills throughout the day. She enjoys talking with patients and that helps put them at ease. In addition, she teaches them important things about their teeth and gums and how to keep them healthy.*

Cynthia describes her job this way:

> You explain to the patients the nature of their cavities and different stages of gum disease. Then you go back, and after you have told them what their problems are, you try to help them find ways to make their gum tissue better. You tell them what types of fillings can be put in different places. If they need crowns or extractions, you tell them how these things are done. We frequently explain root canals, even though we would send a patient needing one to someone else. I sometimes instruct patients on diet, on how to brush their teeth, and on how to floss. If a patient has sore gums, I describe certain kinds of rinses that can make the gums feel better.

## Activities to Improve Your Speaking Skills by Paulette Campbell

Speaking is used daily, in all jobs. These activities will improve your confidence in the speaking skills you have.

**1.** See yourself as others see you. A mirror, especially a full-length one, is a terrific tool for correcting physical distractions that can keep people from hearing what you have to say. Good posture, a pleasant expression, direct eye contact, relaxed arms, and proper placement of your hands while speaking are among the positive, effective bits of body language that can be developed as you study your reflection. All book reports, current events speeches, and class presentations should be practiced in front of a mirror, which becomes a friendly as well as a critical first audience for your speaking endeavor.

**2.** Exercise your tongue just as you would any other muscle you want to condition. The world of literature has a wealth of challenges for getting a lazy tongue into shape. From any work of Shakespeare (Hamlet's monologue that begins "Speak the speech, I pray you" naturally comes to mind) or passages from the King James version of the Bible to Robert Southey's "The Cataract of Lodore," you can design a vocal workout that should be committed to memory and become part of your daily routine. Also, tongue twisters, such as the familiar "She sells seashells down by the seashore" and "Fuzzy Wuzzy wasn't fuzzy, was he?" can be fun as well as functional.

**3.** Sing! Sing! Sing! Church choirs and choral groups are wonderful for learning the basics of breathing properly and projecting your voice. You may never be asked to sing for the Metropolitan Opera, but the aspects of vocal technique and training that you acquire can help you maintain control of your voice, particularly when your nerves threaten to sabotage an important job interview. Also, singing need not be done in front of an audience. The shower provides incredible acoustics, and singing along with a car radio is, more and more, a common everyday occurrence. The point is to create natural opportunities for using your voice in an expressive, non-monotone way.

**4.** Eavesdrop on yourself. When talking on the phone, have a tape recorder running nearby. Then play back the tape and listen to yourself. Just as a mirror can detect physical problems that may affect your speaking effectiveness, a tape recorder can spotlight and help correct vocal imperfections. In addition to the natural instances of conversation, a tape recorder can capture and enhance whatever vocal workout you choose, whether it be soliloquy or scales. Remember, the way your ears hear your voice is not the way everyone else hears it.

**5.** Practice the Scout motto and "Be Prepared." Just as actors rehearse for a play, you should always go over what you plan to say in any public speaking situation. A list of things to be sure to cover is especially helpful, whether asking for a date to the prom or reporting to a social studies class on "The End of the Cold War." Improvisation, or "making it up as you go along," can be dangerous for the unskilled and may lead you to say things you never meant to say or that were better left unsaid. An air of confidence and being sure of oneself can be enhanced by careful planning and rehearsal, even to anticipating possible questions and framing appropriate answers to them.

**6.** Read aloud every chance you get. This could mean reading stories to younger brothers and sisters or to children that you baby-sit for. It also means reading assignments aloud, from chapters in a textbook to *Moby Dick*. Poetry in particular has been written to be heard, just as plays have been. And hearing the words as well as seeing them can add to your comprehension and perhaps even improve your test scores. Increasing the amount you read has other benefits as well. By reading the daily newspaper and newsmagazines like *Time* and *Newsweek*, you not only increase your vocabulary, but also the number of things you have to talk about.

**7.** Put yourself in the other guy's shoes. With a friend or a small group, it is helpful to role play your audience as well as rehearse whatever speaking situation you may face. Too often we forget that a teacher or prospective employer is just another person like ourselves. Role playing can take some of the fear, mystery, and discomfort out of those times when you find it necessary to speak for yourself.

**8.** Audition for a play or run for class office. The more you put yourself in situations that require speaking in front of a group, whether strangers or acquaintances, the better at it you will become. The old adage "Practice makes perfect" works, especially when you do a little self-assessment after each occasion and determine what your strengths were as well as what you need to improve on.

**9.** Take drama or speech classes in your school or community theater. These classes will provide you even more opportunities for public speaking as well as some helpful feedback. Former drama students have used the skills they learned in such wide-ranging professions as psychiatry, politics, nursing, and the ministry.

**Paulette Campbell** has performed as Mrs. Guppy the Magic Clown, taught drama at Needham Broughton High School in Raleigh, North Carolina, produced a children's theater troupe called the Gingerbread Players, and owned the Abracadabra Cafe and Theatre. Having observed firsthand how participation in speech classes and theater activities has affected former students' success in such careers as psychiatry, sales, broadcasting, and the ministry, she is an enthusiastic promoter of training and experience in speech communication.

## LISTENING SKILLS

You will spend most of your working day communicating with others—people over the telephone, co-workers, customers, and your supervisor. Your ability to communicate — through reading, writing, speaking, and listening—will determine your job success. *Only the knowledge of your job is more important than communication skills in predicting your job success.*

Employers value communication skills. They know that such skills are at the heart of getting and keeping customers, and of workers working together as a team.

Of the time the average worker spends communicating, most frequent activities are speaking (23%) and listening (55%). Here are the listening skills you need:

1. Listen carefully to what a person says, noting tone of voice and other body language to understand the content and feelings being expressed.

2. Respond to what a person says in a way that shows your understanding of what is said.

To illustrate this, let's visit with Mitchell Ward. She is a bank vice president and regional personnel manager. She supervises the hiring, firing, promotions, and pay for the people employed by her bank in two states. She obviously knows a great deal and is someone to whom we should give our full attention.

Mitchell, right, speaks to Jenny Joyner after carefully listening to her.

LJ:     How important is listening in your job, Mitchell?

Mitchell: Listening to people is probably the most important thing I do in my whole job. Much of my contact with people is by phone, because my group is very spread out. I have to rely on the telephone a lot, because we have a rather restricted travel budget.

You really have to learn to listen intently to what people say in order to try and do what is in that person's best interest. For example, somebody will say to me, "I am really unhappy in my job, I really want to do something else." Then my next 10 contacts with that person may be by phone talking about different job opportunities that have become available. So it is a constant talking by phone, listening to what they say and asking, "Are you interested in this job? Why aren't you interested in this job?"

Listening to people is extremely important because I have to try and cycle through the information I am getting and figure out what they are telling me. I have to listen intently and then ask those very important questions that will get me the right answers. Listening is important in everything I do. I can't make many mistakes.

LJ:     Do you use any listening techniques?

Mitchell: I ask a lot of open-ended questions, like "Can you tell me more about that?" There are certain techniques I learned to practice over time. For example, nodding one's head will usually encourage a person to talk. I have learned never to be afraid of silence. And when I am communicating with people, I try to give them the sense that I am willing to talk about anything, that no subject is really taboo if they want to talk about it. Below are two other examples of how listening skills are used on the job.

**LAW ENFORCEMENT OFFICER.** *The officer listens to complaints in a conflict between neighbors. The officer learns the facts behind the dispute and mediates it based on these facts, listening carefully to each party.*

**LICENSED PRACTICAL NURSE.** *The LPN talks with patients being admitted to the hospital or clinic. The nurse asks the patient a set of questions, including personal history and present complaints. If needed, additional questions may be asked to draw a clearer picture of the person's problems. After listening to the responses, the nurse records them on a form.*

## Activities to Improve Your Listening Skills by Nancy Banks

*Try the first eight activities with a partner.*

1. Ask your partner to select a sample object or design for you to draw without seeing it as you carefully listen to his or her specific directions. Compare your final product with the original. Practice this activity several times, each time with a different object or design.

2. Ask your partner to dictate a sentence of 15 to 20 words, reading it aloud only twice. Write the sentence from memory and compare it with the original. Practice this activity until you can write longer sentences accurately.

3. Choose a television sitcom for both you and your partner to watch. At the end, briefly summarize the plot, including the major characters and their roles in the story. Ask your partner to critique your summary. You may also want to practice this with a newscast.

4. Ask your partner to read aloud a paragraph from a news article or story, then ask your partner specific questions about the content. Practice this activity often.

5. Practice active listening as your partner describes his or her feelings about a situation. Summarize the feelings experienced without being judgmental.

6. Ask your partner to relate all his or her activities of the previous day. Listen carefully and summarize.

7. Ask your partner to treat you as his or her doctor or nurse and to explain the symptoms of an imaginary illness. Listen and summarize the symptoms accurately.

8. Ask your partner to list 10 unrelated objects in the house for you to remember in sequence. As the words are called, listen carefully; after one minute, repeat the

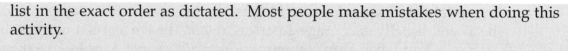

list in the exact order as dictated. Most people make mistakes when doing this activity.

Now listen to the same list a second time, using this memory association trick from *The Memory Book* (1974) by Harry Lorayne and Jerry Lucas. As you listen, associate a ridiculous picture of the first object in relation to the next one on the list. (Example: 1. spoon, 2. desk, 3. telephone—Visualize hundreds of spoons dancing on top of your desk. Then picture your desk answering the phone. The sillier the image, the better.) Continue through the list, linking each word in an absurd manner to the next one. You should be able to repeat the list both forward and backward as you recall the logical associations you made. Days later you will still remember the list.

Next, try including abstract words among the list of objects. (Examples: happiness, hunger, anxiety.) Practice this activity until you can create images rapidly. Apply this trick to lists you need to learn in school.

*Ask your teacher if you can do the classroom activities that follow.*

**9.** With a partner, discuss several of the following: your favorite movie, television program, sport, vacation, book, food, hobby, and pet. Share your partner's preferences with the class.

**10.** At the end of class, summarize, either orally or in writing, the main points of the lesson.

**11.** Listen to two students give opposite opinions about a problem or world situation. Then, impartially summarize what each said.

*Do the following activity on your own.*

**12.** How many times have you talked with someone and realized, "This person is really not listening to me!" Signs of not listening include not making eye contact, yawning, interrupting, looking at one's watch, or responding by talking about something else. Strong listening skills build friendships. They are also essential for an adult—whether listening to a family member, a friend, a co-worker, a boss, or a customer. Here are several listening techniques that will help you.

a. *Use appropriate body language.* Face the person squarely, lean forward, and give appropriate eye contact. You want your body to communicate, "I'm with you; I want to hear what you say."

b. *Restate the thoughts or feelings of the person you are listening to.* This shows that you are truly listening, and it will help you better understand the person. For example, you might respond by saying, "What I hear you saying is . . . .", or "It sounds like you are feeling . . . ."

c. *Ask open-ended questions.* Learn to ask questions that cannot be answered with one or two words, like "Yes" or "No." Some examples: "Can you tell me more about that?," "How did the party go?," "How would you do that?," "What bothers you about that?," or "How did you feel afterwards?"

d. *Use silence.* At times it is often best to listen attentively, and not say anything. This gives the person time to express him or herself without feeling hurried.

Through experience you will learn when it is appropriate to use these techniques. Keep in mind that good listening requires effort, concentration, and skill. Choose one of the techniques and try it out with a friend. Do you see a difference in how he or she responds? After you have mastered when and how to use one technique, choose another one to work on.

**13.** Many schools have peer counseling or peer mediation programs. These programs offer excellent training in listening skills. Why not join one?

**Nancy Banks** is a veteran teacher who considers teenagers both a challenge and a joy. At LeRoy Martin Middle School in Raleigh, North Carolina, she taught language arts, social studies, creative writing, poetry, and electives for the academically gifted. Nancy has received numerous awards for her teaching excellence, including North Carolina Outstanding English Teacher of the Year.

## THINGS YOU CAN DO

Now that you know what the Basic Skills are, you may ask yourself, "How strong am I in these skills? Do I need to work on any of these skills? If so, which ones?" To answer these questions, I have prepared a rating sheet on the next page that will help you rate how strong you are in these skills. Photocopy it and then rate yourself. You can then keep it, and put it in your job skills portfolio (see Chapter 16).

Use the form below and rate yourself. Use your ratings to decide which skills you need to strengthen. Then, do some of the strength building activities listed in this chapter.

## MY SELF-ESTIMATES FOR THE BASIC SKILLS

NAME _____

DATE _____

Rate yourself for each of the skills listed below. Compare yourself with other persons your age. Be sure to read the description of the skill carefully. Circle the appropriate number and *avoid rating yourself the same on each skill.*

**READING:** Identify relevant facts; locate information in books/manuals; find meaning of unknown words; judge accuracy of reports; use computer to find information.

HIGH   8   7   6   5   4   3   2   1   LOW

**WRITING:** Write ideas completely and accurately in letters and reports with proper grammar, spelling, and punctuation; use computer to communicate information.

HIGH   8   7   6   5   4   3   2   1   LOW

**MATHEMATICS:** Use numbers, fractions, and percentages to solve problems; use tables, graphs, and charts; use computer to enter, retrieve, change, and communicate numerical information.

HIGH   8   7   6   5   4   3   2   1   LOW

**SPEAKING:** Speak clearly; select language, tone of voice, and gestures appropriate to audience.

HIGH   8   7   6   5   4   3   2   1   LOW

**LISTENING:** Listen carefully to what person says, tone of voice, and body language; respond in a way that shows understanding of what is said.

HIGH   8   7   6   5   4   3   2   1   LOW

# The Thinking Skills

**W**ork is rapidly changing from what it once was. In the past, there was the boss and those who followed his or her orders. Today, more and more work is done in teams. As the supervisor, or boss, your job is to get everyone to work as a team. Everyone on the team works to produce the best product or service at the lowest cost possible. That means everyone on the team is expected to be a problem solver, decision maker, and idea creator. Whether you are the supervisor or supervisee, you will need thinking skills—skills in creative thinking, decision making, problem solving, and visualization. You will be expected to recognize and define problems, invent solutions, think of better ways of operating, and devise new products or services.

In this chapter, you will learn what these thinking skills are, how they are used at work, and how you can better learn them.

## CREATIVE THINKING SKILLS

Through study and training you can strengthen your creative abilities, and these skills will be important to you in your future work. You will be able to come up with fresh ideas, novel ways of solving problems, and creative ways of doing your work better. All workers will need the following two skills:

1. Using imagination freely, combining ideas or information in new ways.

2. Making connections between ideas that seem unrelated.

How is creative thinking used in the workplace? To understand the use of these skills, we will look in two areas: banking, and teaching young children.

**REAL ESTATE BANKER.** *David Klinge, pictured below, is vice president and real estate banking manager for a large bank. One of his main duties is figuring out how the bank can lend money to companies that build things like shopping centers and office buildings. Money can be lent in different ways. For example, let's say a company wants to build a sports stadium. The bank might lend the money to build it, but when it is finished, the loan ends, and the bank's loan is paid off. But where does the money come from to pay the bank? From another loan that the builder gets from someone else, such as an insurance company. It's David's job to come up with a creative way of putting all these pieces together, so the bank can make a deal.*

**David Klinge doesn't go through a day without using creative thinking and problem-solving skills in this position.**

**EARLY CHILDHOOD TEACHERS.** *Teachers use creative thinking to find effective ways for their students to learn. I talked with two teachers at the Campus Child Care Center who are good examples of this: Patricia (Patty) Judd and assistant teacher Ireland Stanton. You can see them working together to plan their lessons in the photo on the next page.*

LJ:     Tell me what your jobs are.

Patty:  I am one of three teachers in our room. I am the middle teacher, and I assist and help plan and work with the children.

Ireland: I am the assistant teacher and I assist Patty inside the classroom—whatever is needed, from planning to changing a diaper.

**Ireland Stanton, left, and Patty Judd discuss what they will teach next week.**

LJ:       You plan, together, what you will be doing with the students—is that right?

Patty:   We try to have one day a week when we sit down and get all our books out and plan and think of a theme, think of ideas of art and dramatic play and cooking activities.

LJ:       What would be an example of a theme that you might plan a class around?

Ireland: Sharing, self-esteem, playing together.  Also, we go to the libraries and get books about whatever theme we are covering.

LJ:       What is a theme that you have done recently?

Patty:   Last week was fall colors and fall foods.

LJ:       What would be some activities that you thought up together?

Ireland: We made apple betty in the classroom for the kids.  They did it actually.  We measured out the flour, sugar, nutmeg, and cinnamon, but they poured it in and mixed it.  The teachers cut the apples and we all placed it in a pan, baked it, and ate it for an afternoon snack.  They got a feel of what it is like to cook.  Patty had pumpkin seeds the week before and the kids loved them.  They learned that out of a pumpkin comes seeds that can be washed, put in a pan with a little oil and salt, baked in an oven, and eaten.  Working with the seeds was fun for the kids.

LJ:       What is it that you hope the students will learn from doing an activity like that?

Patty:   Sharing and working together.

## Activities for Improving Your Creative Thinking by Lorraine Powers

**1.** Shoplifting is a serious problem for many store owners. Create a plan for a store to use to deal with shoplifting. Interview the store owner and identify the strengths and weaknesses of your plan. What did the owner recommend? As an alternative, you could suggest to your teacher that a store owner be invited in to give a presentation to the class on shoplifting; you and your classmates could then develop plans based on this.

**2.** Create a game to increase your problem-solving skills. For example, create a board game with a series of problem cards and solution cards. Players advance game pieces by rolling dice, landing on spaces on the game board, and selecting a problem and solution cards. The winner is the first person to reach an objective. What TV game shows or existing board games could be modified to make a problem-solving game?

**3.** Spend an afternoon at work with one of your parents or guardians or another adult. Observe their job and identify its key characteristics. What problems did they face? How did they handle their problems? Did they use any creative thinking techniques like "brainstorming"? Summarize your visit and present it to the class.

**4.** Identify a problem at your school—for example, lunch lines, time between classes, tardies, etc. Using a problem-solving method (for example, the scientific method), create a solution to the problem. Document your insights, procedure, problems, and solutions. Present it to your class. Why do you think your solution will work?

**5.** Keep a weekly journal of creative ideas. Each week jot down any problem you have noticed in your environment. Attempt to create an informal solution to the problem. At the end of each nine weeks, go back and read your journal and identify one or two problems you would like to work on and create a solution for them to present to the class. What are the strengths of your solutions? Weaknesses?

**6.** Create a reference file of problem-solving articles. Go to your local library and look up creative thinking and/or problem solving. Collect 10 good articles that describe the process. Put them all together on note cards or in a notebook. Include an introduction explaining how to use your reference file.

**7.** Create a new food item. Write the recipe down including all ingredients and amounts. Bring in a sample for the class. What were some of the problems you encountered when creating a new food item? What do you recommend for overcoming any problems?

**8.** Create a new product for young people your age. It can be any product of your choice: new jeans, a new flavor of soft drink, a new type of candy bar. Bring in a demo or picture of the product to class. Why would someone want to buy your product? What problems would you have with convincing people to buy it (e.g., cost, competition)? If you want to be creative, create an ad or cute jingle for your product.

**Lorraine Powers** is the second of seven children in her family. She has spent her entire life using creativity to play with and educate children. She strongly believes in promoting creative thinking and problem solving. Lorraine is a former marketing education high school teacher and is currently a graduate student working on a doctorate in occupational education. In the future, she plans to do research on creativity and problem solving.

## PROBLEM-SOLVING SKILLS

In your job you will be alert for possible problems. Perhaps you will notice a machine that is likely to break because it is not being taken care of, or an unsafe way that passengers are being handled that might lead to injury and a lawsuit. You will want to develop the skills needed to solve problems like these. You will want to be able to

1. recognize a problem, a gap between what is and what should or could be.

2 identify why it is a problem.

3. create and implement a solution.

4. watch to see how well the solution works and revise it if needed.

Below are some examples of how problem-solving skills are used at work.

**RESEARCH FORESTER.** *Jorge Vasquez's specialty is tropical forestry. As he explains, "I work with a cooperative [called a "co-op"] of companies and North Carolina State University's Department of Forestry that tries to preserve tropical conifers [like pine trees] of Central America and Mexico. Seeds are collected and distributed among co-op members, who plant them in several countries of South America. In some ways, we try to preserve the commercial possibilities of the species of trees [for example, to produce the pulp used in making paper or particle board]."*

*Jorge works on problems related to breeding strategy; that is, deciding which trees to breed. He needs to consider many factors, including the volume of a tree, its shape or form, the soil and weather conditions in which it lives, and its family of origin [for example, its mother and father]. His skills in genetics and mathematics are essential for solving these problems.*

*When I talked with Jorge, he was figuring out the best way to select the trees from which seeds would be taken to grow new trees. He had diagrammed four different ways of doing it, each on a separate piece of paper. You can see him working with the diagrams in the photo on page 76.*

Jorge Vasquez working on possible solutions to the problem of selecting the trees from which to take seeds to grow new trees.

**MARKETING SPECIALIST.** *As a marketing specialist, Pia Lapitus handles the marketing for 30 banking centers. Pia's bank is offering a new deluxe banking program, and Pia and her co-workers must solve a problem concerning the program—which customers of the bank should be eligible for the program? Customers in this deluxe program will receive free checking, travelers cheques, and bank cards. These services cost the bank money. The bank is willing to offer these free to its best customers. In deciding which customers will qualify to join this program, Pia and her co-workers are considering several "qualifiers." For example, if a customer has a $10,000 loan with the bank, will he or she be eligible for the deluxe plan? In considering this idea, Pia must decide if it would be profitable to give such customers all these "freebies."*

Pia Lapitus and her co-workers discuss the possible solutions to a problem.

**CUSTOMER SERVICE REPRESENTATIVE.** *The representative deals with a customer's problem, such as a malfunctioning computer, listening carefully to find out what is wrong (e.g., computer does not have enough memory). The representative explains the problem to the customer, and then writes up the order for additional memory and notifies the sales department of the order.*

## Activities to Strengthen Your Problem-Solving Skills by Dick Peterson

1. Actively look for and identify problems. It can be fun. Is there a product that you use that could be improved? Do you have an idea for a new product that would help someone? Is there something at school that could be changed to improve the environment for both teachers and students? Make a list of the problems you encounter during the day. Do this over a period of several weeks.

2. Form a problem-solving team. It is often helpful to involve many people in the solution of a problem. Sometimes it is difficult to solve a problem by yourself.

3. Read a book or listen to an audiotape about problem solving.

4. Write a statement about a problem. It is helpful to express what the problem is and to write it down. If you can express it clearly, then you can work on a solution. Don't limit your options by defining your problem too narrowly. For example, if your define a problem as building a boat to cross a pond, then your solution will look like a boat. A boat may not always be the best solution. If your definition was to transport something across a body of water then you would be open to many possibilities. A boat may or may not necessarily be the best possibility.

5. Develop a problem-solving action plan. Sometimes problems don't get solved because they are too complex. Breaking down the problem into small tasks can help. What should you do first? Putting all the steps into a plan of action will help to make big problems manageable. Write each step down. Remember to take the first step and follow through with your plan.

6. Talk to a friend. Sometimes the answer comes to you through the process of talking about the problem to others. The expression "let's talk it out" is an example of this approach. Sometimes the other person only has to listen and ask the right questions.

7. Use analogies to solve a problem. Sometimes problems are similar to other things. Imagine what a problem might be like. Could it be like an onion where you can peel away layers to discover new layers? Could it be like a seed that needs water and right conditions to grow? Frederick Kekule imagined that the molecular structure of the benzene ring in chemistry was like a snake. Sometimes solutions to problems can be found by looking at the problem in a unique way. How many different ways can you think of to represent a problem?

8. Research a problem. Often a solution to a problem depends upon finding out as much information as possible about the problem. Do you have enough infor-

mation about the problem? Do you know what the problem really is? Begin by listing everything you know about the problem. Sometimes people do not realize how much information they know about a problem unless they stop and think about it. Ask your friends and tell them you are working on this problem. They may have information that can help or know people who have expertise in the area you are interested in. Collect information and organize it in a useful way before you take action.

**9.** Join Odyssey of the Mind, or OM, an exciting program that you are sure to enjoy. The word "odyssey" means a long wandering or a series of travels, and OM is a trip you don't want to miss. It works like this. You join a team of four to six students like yourself, and you compete with other school teams to see who is best at creative problem solving. There are state, national, and world competitions.

A school becomes a member of OM by joining the OM Association, a not-for-profit corporation. Members come from throughout the U.S., Canada, Europe, Australia, Japan, and China. Talk with your teachers to see if your school is a member and, if not, why not join? For additional information, contact Odyssey of the Mind, P.O. Box 547, Glassboro, NJ 08028.

**Dick Peterson** is an associate professor of technology education at North Carolina State University. Creative problem solving has been an emphasis of his work since 1982. He is actively involved with the Odyssey of the Mind creative problem-solving program. He has worked with students and teachers from elementary school through college to promote creative problem-solving activities. Dr. Peterson became interested in problem solving as a student in college. A teacher challenged him to look at problems in different ways and to consider all possibilities in arriving at a solution.

## DECISION-MAKING SKILLS

Everyday at work you will make many decisions—decisions that affect the organization for which you work, and decisions that affect your future happiness. It is important, therefore, that you become an effective decision maker.

Today, we know a great deal about how to make good decisions. Most important, we know that a good decision is an *informed* decision. Consequently, in making a decision you want to be able to

1. identify the goal desired in making the decision.

2. generate alternatives for reaching the goal.

3. gather information about the alternatives (e.g., from experts or books).

4. weigh the pros and cons of each alternative (i.e., gains/losses to yourself and others, approval/disapproval of self and others).

5. make the best choice.

6. plan how to carry out your choice and what you will do if negative consequences occur.

Nursing is a good example of an occupation requiring many decisions. In this next interview, we will meet a nurse manager named Alphonso Hayes. As you will see, his work is filled with decisions.

LJ:        Alphonso, what is the name of your position?

Alphonso: I am the assistant nurse manager for the progress care unit. I am a registered nurse. I started as a staff nurse, and now I am at the level of assistant nurse manager.

LJ:        What kinds of duties do you have in this position?

Alphonso: My position involves covering staff positions, meaning that if the nursing staff can't handle the work load then I fill in where I am needed. Also, I function as the charge nurse for the shift I am working on. We have three work shifts, so whatever shift I am working on, I usually function as the charge nurse for that shift. I take responsibility for the functioning of the unit, making sure that everything runs smoothly. That means, for example, that the patients are admitted, relocated, or discharged properly. I see that the staff have adequate materials or equipment or resources to do their job well.

LJ:        What would be an example of something that they might need that you would get?

Alphonso: Sometimes a nurse may have a patient who requires a little more nursing time than they have to give. I will either fill in to help them or see if anyone else can come in and give assistance. I coordinate the care to make sure that things work out okay.

**Alphonso Hayes explains to Audrey Daniel a decision he has made about the nursing staff.**

Below are two additional examples of decision making in the workplace.

**RESTAURANT MANAGER.** *The restaurant manager chooses a restaurant supply company or vendor based upon the quality and value of the food and beverage items it offers. The manager gathers information, compares prices, and decides which vendor to use.*

**EXCAVATING EQUIPMENT OPERATOR.** *The operator determines what kind and size of equipment to use for a project. The operator learns how much dirt is to be dug out, where it is to be dumped, and the time allowed to do it. He or she decides what combination of equipment (e.g., power shovel, bulldozer, dump trucks) will best meet this goal.*

## Activities for Improving Decision-Making Skills by Donna Brenniman

1. You make many decisions each day. To help you understand the number of decisions you make each day, keep a decision-making journal for at least one day. In your journal, record every decision you make, from the clothes you wear to how to best help a friend. Also, record your thoughts about these decisions. At the end of the day, ask yourself the following questions: What were the consequences of my decisions? Did I make the best choice? Could using the decision-making process help me make better decisions in the future?

2. Have you ever wished that you could decide where to go on a field trip? Make a proposal for a field trip that would interest you and your classmates. Decide what you would like to learn about. Next, gather information about possible destinations. Ask a teacher to advise you on all the factors that must be considered when proposing a field trip in your school district. List the positive and negative consequences for each destination you are considering. Write and submit your proposal. Happy travels!

3. Is there a controversial issue in the news that you feel strongly about or one you would like to learn more about? Investigate both sides of the issue. Write down the alternative solutions, including their pros and cons. Take a stand on the issue. Write an editorial that supports your opinion, and send it to the local newspaper. You could also organize a classroom debate on the issue.

4. Create a skit that demonstrates good decision making for elementary students. Be sure the subject of the skit will be useful to younger students. Make arrangements to present your skit at your local elementary school. If it is not convenient for your group to travel to the elementary school, videotape your skit and send the tape to the elementary school.

5. Many television characters deal with issues that may affect you: peer pressure, divorce, dating, friendship, and so on. Watch a popular television show with some friends. Discuss the decisions the characters made at the end of the show. Can you and your friends identify with any of the characters and/or the decisions that they made? Do the decisions television characters make influence your lives? How?

6. Elected officials often make decisions that affect your life, either now or in the future. These officials include school board members, county commissioners, and state or federal legislators. Write or telephone one of them to schedule an

appointment to interview her or him about the decision-making process they use. Ask them what steps they go through in making a decision. Be sure to prepare your questions beforehand. This would also be a good class project.

**Donna Brenniman** is a seventh grade communication skills and social studies teacher in Clayton, North Carolina. She has received two Excellence in Education awards from her county. Her interest in decision making comes from helping her middle school students learn how to overcome the obstacles they face in and out of school. She wrote the activities above, based on her experience in working with students like you.

## Decisional Balance Sheet

I added one more activity that I know you will find helpful. You will learn to use a "decisional balance sheet" to make important decisions. I have found it very helpful. It has six steps.

1. Make or photocopy several decisional balance sheets like the one you see on the next page. Use them to make a decision that is important to you by following the next steps.

2. Ask yourself, "With this decision I am facing, what are my alternatives?" Write down all your options. All the possible solutions. Really brainstorm! Then, select those that look most promising.

3. For each of the best options make out a balance sheet. Write the name of the option at the top. First, write down the ways *you* would gain or lose by this option. Second, write down the ways *others* (e.g., friends or family members) would gain or lose if you chose this option.

   Third, write down how you would feel about yourself if you chose this option. Would you approve of yourself? Or disapprove? And, finally, write down how *others* would feel if you made this choice? Would the people who are important to you approve of you or disapprove of you for making this choice? Write these down in the space provided on the balance sheet.

4. Review your balance sheets and choose the best option.

5. Plan out how you will carry out your decision. Write out the steps you will take.

6. Look again at the balance sheet you made for the option you chose. What are the negative things that might happen? Plan for how you will handle them if they occur.

The decisional balance sheet works well. Give it a try!

**OPTION:** _____

**A.** Gains or losses to myself or others:

GAINS                                                    LOSSES

**B**. Approval or disapproval of myself or others:

APPROVAL                                              DISAPPROVAL

## VISUALIZATION SKILLS

In most jobs, various kinds of diagrams are used to communicate information. A simple example is the map a bus driver uses to learn which streets to travel and where to pick up passengers. These diagrams may be charts, outlines, blueprints, or drawings. They may communicate the steps followed in handling a customer's written complaint, how an electronic circuit works, or how sewage travels through a waste treatment plant. In your work, you must be able to

1. see a building or an object from a blueprint, drawing, or sketch.

2. imagine how a system works by looking at a schematic drawing.

We will look at two examples of industries that use visualization skills: banking and dentistry.

**REAL ESTATE BANKER.** *We met David Klinge earlier in this chapter when we were discussing creative thinking. In this section, we will see how he and his co-workers—Marie Stapleton and Brent Farnham—use visualization skills.*

*When deciding whether to lend money to a company that wants to build something, like an office building, David and his co-workers need to fully understand how it is going to be built. They need to know where the building is going to be located on the property, where the sidewalks and streets are going to be, and so on. They can learn this from a blueprint, a precise drawing that shows where these things will be. In the photo below, you can see on the table the blueprints for an office building.*

Brent, Marie, and David discuss what the office building will look like.

In the next photo (on page 84), you can see Marie pointing to the outline (darker line) of the office building on the blueprint. If you look closely, you can see where the parking lot will be, to the right of the building.

**Marie points to the outline of the office building on the blueprint.**

**DENTISTRY.** *Dentists, dental assistants, and dental hygienists use visualization skills when examining X-rays of teeth. In the photo below, Cynthia Wilson, a registered dental hygienist, and Eileen Kestle, a certified dental assistant, examine an X-ray of a patient's teeth. When they see on the X-ray a place where a tooth is decaying, they are able to visualize where that tooth is in the patient's mouth. They are easily able to find the spot.*

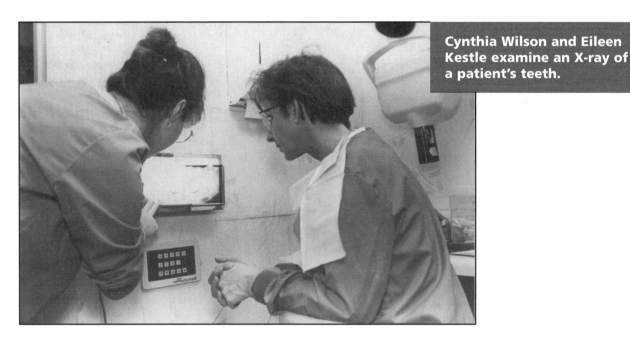

**Cynthia Wilson and Eileen Kestle examine an X-ray of a patient's teeth.**

They also use their visualization skills with a periodontal chart (see example on page 85). The perio chart is like a blueprint of the mouth. The dentist marks on it such things as decay, fillings, cavities, root canals, and so on. Dentistry professionals can look at one of these charts and visualize the teeth in a patient's mouth.

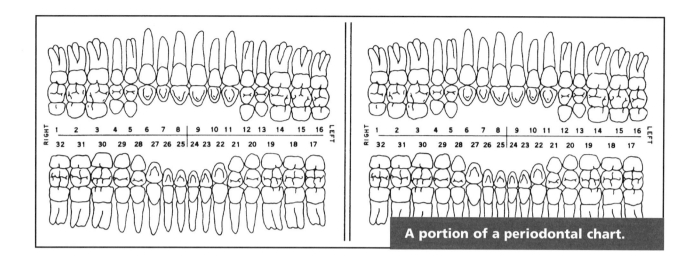

**A portion of a periodontal chart.**

## Activities for Developing Visualization Skills by Alice Scales

**1.** Draw a road map from your house to your school from memory. Add street names and landmarks.

**2.** Assemble items that come unassembled or partially assembled using the diagram that comes with it. The best source for these are models such as space ships, boats, cars, and airplanes.

**3.** Play computer games that require you to fit objects together or rotate objects into new positions.

**4.** Place a number of basic solid shapes (cubes, cones, pyramids, cylinders, etc.) into an opaque paper or plastic bag. Next, stick your hand into the plastic bag so that you cannot see the objects, and feel each shape with your fingers. Describe and name each shape you feel, and then draw out that object to see how close you came to determining the shape.

**5.** Measure the length of the walls in your bedroom, and draw a diagram of its shape on 1/4" or 1/8" grid paper allowing one block to equal 1' or 1/2'. Be sure to show where windows and doors are located, and indicate the directions that doors swing. Next, measure the width and depth of each piece of furniture in your bedroom. Now, using the same grid paper you used to layout your room, cut pieces of paper the size and shape of each piece of your furniture. Place the furniture pieces on the grid layout of your room and try different furniture arrangements that will give you more space or a more attractive room. With each new arrangement, mentally stroll around the room imagining how the room will look. Try to imagine if you will have any problems with the arrangement. Will drawers and doors hit other objects? Will you be able to easily make your bed? Use the same approach described above to rearrange a classroom so students have a larger or more efficient space to work.

**6.** Locate books on technical illustration in your library or book store and read the information on how light, shape, and material affects the look of objects. Read the information on techniques for drawing them, and try some of the techniques yourself.

**7.** Design a new student desk for your classroom that has a built-in book rack and places for pencils, pens, markers, and storage for paper. The desk should still have plenty of room to work, and can be made out of any material and configuration, but must be totally different from the desk you see in schools. Now, try to adapt the design of the desk to include a small computer station that allows students to have both a nice work area for reading and writing, and easy access to the computer with room to use the keyboard and move around a mouse.

**8.** Obtain books on laying out and reading blueprints from your school or local library. Select a floor plan of a house and construct a scale model of it. The model can be made out of any material, such as sheet Styrofoam, cardboard, wood, or a combination of materials. Next, design your dream house on 1/4"or 1/8" grid paper letting one block equal 1 foot. Look at plans in magazines and books for inspiration. Walk through you dream house mentally. Try to look for advantages and disadvantages in your plans. Will doors hit each other? Can you move furniture in and out of your house easily? Are the bedrooms far enough from the rest of the house so that someone could take a nap without being awakened by noise from the television? Redesign the plan to solve problems you find.

Alice Scales teaches graphic communications at North Carolina State University. She previously taught the middle grades, high school, and in a hospital. She has degrees in science education and industrial arts education. Not many women teach industrial arts (IA), but Alice is a third-generation IA teacher. She originally took classes in industrial arts as a whim and liked it better than science. She highly recommends that girls take courses in technical fields.

For more about industrial arts, or what is often called exploring technology, turn to page 176 where you will get a closer look at these types of courses.

## THINGS YOU CAN DO

Just as in the last chapter, I have created a rating scale to estimate your skill strengths. This scale is for your thinking skills. Make a photocopy and rate yourself. Use your ratings to decide which thinking skills you need to work on. Then, do the activities listed for your weaker skills.

Record the activities you complete on the form at the end of Chapter 16, and be sure to put your rating sheet in your job skills portfolio (see also Chapter 16).

## MY SELF-ESTIMATES FOR THE THINKING SKILLS

NAME _____

DATE _____

Rate yourself for each of the skills listed below. Compare yourself with other persons your age. Be sure to read the description of the skill if you are unsure what it means. Circle the appropriate number and *avoid rating yourself the same on each skill.*

**CREATIVE THINKING:** Use imagination freely, combining ideas or information in new ways; make connections between ideas that seem unrelated.

HIGH   8   7   6   5   4   3   2   1   LOW

**PROBLEM-SOLVING SKILLS:** Recognize problems; identify why it is a problem; create and implement a solution; watch to see how well the solution works; revise as needed.

HIGH   8   7   6   5   4   3   2   1   LOW

**DECISION-MAKING SKILLS:** Identify goal; generate alternatives and gather information about them; weigh pros and cons; choose best alternative; plan how to carry out choice.

HIGH   8   7   6   5   4   3   2   1   LOW

**VISUALIZATION:** Imagine building, object, or system by looking at a blueprint or drawing.

HIGH   8   7   6   5   4   3   2   1   LOW

# CHAPTER 8

## The People Skills

In your job, you will be in daily contact with people, whether the public or your co-workers or team members. There will be conflicts between people and conflicts between different departments. Many of the people you work with will be different from you in appearance and cultural background. You will work to see that your team succeeds. You will need people skills: social skills, and skills in negotiation, leadership, teamwork, and handling cultural diversity. You will learn about these skills in this chapter.

### SOCIAL SKILLS

Whether you are talking with a customer, a co-worker, or your boss—you will need to master the following social skills:

1. Show understanding, friendliness, and respect for the feelings of others.

2. Assert oneself when appropriate. This means standing up for yourself and your ideas in a firm, positive way.

3. Take an interest in what people say and do, and why they think and act as they do.

Below are a number of examples showing how these social skills are used at work.

**LICENSED PRACTICAL NURSE.** *The LPN talks in a caring way with the family members of a sick patient. The LPN responds in a polite and understanding way when family members make frequent calls for information, understands the family's needs and helps them as much as he or she can, and teaches family members how to take care of patient at home, such as how to change bandages.*

**PROFESSOR.** *Lope Max Díaz is a gifted teacher who loves teaching. In the photo below you see him in his "Design Fundamentals" class talking with Meredith Bagerski about the art work she has created.*

Professor Díaz talks with Meredith Bagerski about a piece she has created for the class.

Teaching requires well-developed social skills. Lope challenges his students to think critically and to express themselves. At the same time, he is sensitive to their needs and encourages them.

**HAIRSTYLIST.** *A hairstylist must show understanding, friendliness, empathy, and courtesy to clients. The hairstylist listens carefully to what a customer has to say and answers in a friendly way, suggests ideas to the customer about possible hairstyles and beauty treatments, and assumes the customer is usually right in decisions unless the customer's ideas are too "extreme" to be practical. If the customer's ideas are impractical, the hairstylist suggests, in a friendly way, alternatives for the customer to consider.*

## Activities for Developing Social Skills by Becky Watson

**1.** Often when our friends are having difficult times, we want to let them know that we understand what they are going through. When a friend has made an achievement we also want to share our excitement for them. Attempting to select a greeting card for someone is difficult when you are trying to find the right thing to say. Frequently, greeting cards are plentiful for celebrations and special occasions, but difficult to find for personal occasions, especially painful ones. Often the best approach is to design your own card. Drug stores have machines for this purpose. You can also design a card using a computer, or create one from art materials. Design a card to give to a friend. Perhaps he or she has lost a favorite pet, scored the winning points in a conference game, was suspended from school for smoking, or lost a girlfriend or boyfriend to a best friend. Showing our concern and interest in our friends is very important.

**2.** Planning celebrations for your best friends takes effort, but you usually know what will be successful. However, planning a celebration for people that you don't know can be difficult. With a few of your friends, plan a celebration for someone in a nursing home, some young children, or some handicapped persons living in a group home. Remember that you need to see the event from their perspective and what they might enjoy, not from yours.

**3.** Pen pals have always been an avenue to learn about people in other states or countries. The problem with this communication, however, is that often the letters travel slowly and we lose interest in the project. E-mail, however, is an instant way to connect with friends from other areas. Often friends who live far away can become best friends with frequent communication. We can share more about ourselves in this manner. Being a good pal is a responsibility. Promoting the relationship requires responding in a supportive way to persons we have never met.

**4.** Often young adults have an idea of a career they would like to pursue, but have no understanding of what type of preparation must be made in advance so that the career will be available to them. Discuss with your friends what types of occupations you would like to pursue. Then make appointments with workers in these fields for an interview. Prepare your interview questions in advance. Ask the worker if you can tape your session. In the interview session, ask the person why he or she chose that line of work, and what young people could do to prepare themselves for this occupation. Make a collection of these tapes for the guidance department at your school.

**5.** Teenagers become bored in the summertime, and community service organizations always need volunteers. Isn't there some way that the two can get together? Make a list of all the community services in your area that need summertime volunteers. You will need to call these organizations to find out what type of volunteers they need. Design a poster that will advertise these agencies. Ask businesspersons if you can place the signs in their windows.

**6.** Some people need to have their most frequently called numbers printed in large letters and numbers. Make a telephone directory for emergency or helpful numbers that an elderly or sight impaired person might need. Print the directory on the computer using large point type, laminate your product, and provide a magnet for attachment to the refrigerator. Distribute the list to community agencies that serve the elderly and sight impaired.

**7.** Spending money has always been a problem for teenagers. You have decided that many of your clothes and toys are no longer useful, so you and your friends plan a yard sale. Decide on a specific amount of money to be asked for each item that you have included. Decide ahead of time how little you will take if you have an interested buyer. Decide on the merits of each item and how you will bargain with the potential buyer for a higher price.

**8.** Listen to motivational speeches. You encounter them in church, on television, and in literature. Decide why the person has spoken in that way. Determine a topic that you feel very strongly about. Design a motivational speech that will persuade others to see your point of view. Use a thesaurus to find words that are powerful persuaders.

**9.** "People watching" can often be an enjoyable pastime. Videotape people on a busy street, or in your mall. As you watch your video at home, try to decide what the occupations, hobbies, or interests are of the people you see. Write a profile of each person. Compare your ideas with a friend. Justify why you think the way you do about each person. When you make your videotape be aware that some people may not want their picture taken. It's a good idea to videotape in a way that people are unlikely to notice, and don't tape anyone who objects.

**10.** Make suggestions to your scout leader, church youth leader, or recreation center director about how your program can be improved. Offer to design a survey and report the results.

**Becky Watson** is a doctoral student at North Carolina State University where she teaches people interested in entering the field of teaching. At NCSU she received the Graduate Student Award for Outstanding Teaching and is a member of the Phi Delta Kappa honor society for educators. Becky has been a teacher in the elementary and middle grades. Becky also managed a private company for 10 years and learned "what it takes" to succeed in business. According to Becky, "Social skills are very important. People in business must be able to understand the perspective of the 'customer,' and all people must be able to 'sell themselves or their ideas.' Being forceful, yet empathic, is another important ability."

## NEGOTIATION SKILLS

Whenever people get together, conflicts seem inevitable. For example, if you were organizing a baseball team of your classmates, isn't it likely that more that one person would want to play the same position, like pitcher? Or, when you try to find a time to practice, isn't it likely that one time is good for some people, but not for others?

At work you will find conflicts arising between individuals, departments, and organizations. How do you resolve these conflicts?

There are unsatisfactory ways of resolving them. For example, some people resolve conflicts through threats of force, "Give me that, or I'll . . . ." I'm sure you have seen "bullies" act in this way. In contrast, some people will say "Yes" in almost every situation because they fear conflict. Both methods lead to resentment and ill-will. They are inappropriate in the workplace.

A better way of handling conflict is to negotiate. Negotiation is a valuable skill. All workers need it. You will want to be able to

1.  identify the common goals among different parties in conflict and the ways they depend on each other.

2.  clearly present the facts and arguments of your own position.

3.  listen to and understand the other party's position.

4.  create and propose possible options for resolving the conflict, making reasonable compromises.

Below are some examples of how negotiation skills are used in the workplace.

**OFFICE MANAGER.** *The office manager helps employees work out a solution to a conflict. The manager helps each person understand the other's point of view and work out a compromise.*

**MATERIALS MANAGER AND PURCHASING AGENTS.** *Negotiation skills are important ones to have at Exide Electronics, particularly in the purchasing department. This company makes electric power systems. The company purchases large quantities of materials like wire, copper, and electronic parts to build these systems. There are three purchasing agents who buy these materials. It's the purchasing agents' job to get the best deal for Exide. For example, when the agents buy copper wire, they contact a number of companies that make this wire to find out what their price is and how soon they can deliver it. Based on what the agent learns, he or she negotiates the best deal for the company.*

Sarah Wenzel, Sandra Greene, Peter Underhill, and Michele Wysocki discuss strategies for buying the part Sandra is holding.

## Activities for Developing Negotiation Skills by Wetonah Rice Parker

**1.** A good way to improve your negotiation skills is to have actual practice. Check with your school counselor or an administrator about becoming involved in a peer mediation [see p. 168] or conflict resolution program. If your school does not have one, ask about other organizations in your community, church, town, or city that have developed programs to mediate conflicts among teens.

**2.** Think of a conflict at home, or when you were working or playing with friends, or at school that you feel you did not handle well. Re-create the incident in your mind, write down what happened, and think of reasons why it was not resolved (in your opinion) satisfactorily. What common goals did you share with the other individual(s)? If you had the same conflict today, how would you handle it differently so that you could feel good about the outcome?

**3.** How do you handle your anger? Do you get angry when you do not get your way or when someone says something that you do not agree with? Negotiations require a "cool" head. A good strategy to practice is to talk to yourself to keep "a lid" on your anger. How do you practice talking to yourself without looking silly? Here are some steps you can practice:

a. Say silently to yourself, "Stay calm. It is important that I stay calm as I talk and present my case."

b. Stay focused on the issue. Keep reminding yourself, "What is the actual problem? How are we going to solve it?" Clearly present the facts and arguments of your position.

c. If you find yourself "losing it," you may want to step away from the discussion, both mentally and physically, to calm down. Maybe a minute or two of several deep breaths or counting to 10 (or above) will help you put everything back into perspective. Then, continue with the discussion.

d. Do not forget the art of the compromise. A little give-and-take can be a good way to resolve conflicts between people.

**4.** Good negotiators do their homework. The more information you have about an issue or a situation, the better equipped you will be to negotiate. Use the library to research your subject before negotiating. Learn to ask questions and clearly present the facts and arguments of your own position. Not doing this will cause you to be at a disadvantage. You can be sure that others have done their homework and will be prepared. And, if they haven't, they will marvel at your wealth of knowledge!

**5.** Negotiators succeed by having good listening skills. Practice listening to words that your parents, teachers, siblings, and friends say. Listen for the way they say things, the tone, the phrasing, and, most important, observe the way they look when they are talking. While you are listening, keep an open mind. Encourage the individual to keep talking by nodding your head, saying "uh, uh" or "Right," and asking for clarification of points by saying, "I understand you to say that. . ." or "Do you mean that. . .?" Clarification gives others the chance to repeat the statement(s) and to make a point clearer. Also, it gives you an opportunity to be sure that you heard it right the first time!

**6.** Flea markets and yard sales are great places to practice your negotiation skills. If you find something you want to buy, try to engage in friendly "haggling" for a better price. Make an offer for the item (below the price asked) and negotiate with the seller until you reach an agreement.

**7.** Some communities have an *ombudsman*, resolution services to help settle disputes, and/or mediation services available to the public. In addition, some attorneys specialize in mediation services. Check your telephone book or call the office of the district attorney or the magistrate and inquire whether or not these services are available. If your community has these services, try to arrange an interview with someone in the office. Be sure you have definite questions to ask: What type of training is necessary? What kinds of cases are mediated? What techniques are most commonly used?

**8.** More and more videotapes and books on negotiation and mediation are appearing. Check with your school or public library to see what they have. Negotiation videos for grades 4-12 include *When You're Mad! Mad! Mad!*, *Dealing with Anger*, and *Mediation: Getting to Win Win*. Here is a book available from your local bookstore, *Mediation for Kids*, by Fran Schmidt. So, read, view, and practice!

**Wetonah Rice Parker** is well acquainted with how tempers can flare among students, after 14 years of teaching in middle school. She understands that when "cooler heads prevail" in a conflict situation, everyone involved is more satisfied with the outcome. Dr. Parker is currently an assistant professor of education at Meredith College, Raleigh, North Carolina, where she works with students who want to teach.

## LEADERSHIP SKILLS

Today's workers are *both* leaders and followers. In the past, most workers were passive followers: they waited for orders from their boss and then followed them. They were responsible only for what they were told to do. Today, workers look beyond the work they do themselves. They consider how well everyone and everything is working. If another worker needs help in learning, they help her or him. They alert their supervisors to potential problems and offer suggestions for improving how the work is done. They set a good example for the other workers.

For example, if, as a worker, you saw that the parts your department needs are going to be delayed, you would tell your supervisor and perhaps offer a suggestion for how this could be avoided in the future. You might also suggest what work can be done until the parts arrive, so everyone can keep working. By being a leader, you help your organization offer the best product or service at the lowest possible cost.

You need the following leadership skills:

1. Communicate thoughts and feelings to justify a position.

2. Encourage, persuade, or convince individuals or groups.

3. Make positive use of rules or values followed by others. For example, many organizations use "Robert's Rules of Order" to conduct their business meetings. A good leader knows how to use rules like these so there can be a productive meeting. In addition, he or she knows what the organization values, like quality service to customers, and uses those values in a positive way to influence others.

4. Exhibit ability to have others believe in and trust you due to your competence and honesty.

Below are ways these skills are actually used at work.

**RESTAURANT MANAGER.** *The restaurant manager motivates waiters and waitresses to achieve and maintain high standards of customer service, despite the negative aspects of the job. The manager listens to the complaints of workers about rude or unpleasant customers and offers suggestions and encourages them to provide good service.*

**ENVIRONMENTAL SERVICES SUPERVISOR.** *Willie Plummer has a critical job at Durham Regional Hospital; he supervises the 16 to 20 employees who keep the hospital clean and sanitary. In the photo below, he is talking with one of them, Patty Graham.*

Willie Plummer develops a good relationship with the people he supervises so that they can work together as an effective team to keep the hospital clean and sanitary.

Willie is responsible for scheduling when his people work, seeing that they are properly trained, keeping up their morale, and checking to see that they are doing their jobs properly. When you think about the illnesses that people bring to the hospital and the need for sanitary conditions for people having surgery, you realize how important the work of Willie and his people is.

LJ:     What things do you do to keep morale up and keep your people performing the way they're supposed to?

Willie:  One of the first things you have to do is to give them time to get to know you. You don't push too hard, and you need to get to know each employee as an individual. Each one has a different attitude and personality. Everybody has a bad day sometimes. When they have a bad day you need to know how to maneuver around that. I try to find their good side to keep them motivated.

**BANK COMMUNITY INVESTMENT COORDINATOR.** *Rodney Hood is a leader in our business community. I interviewed him along with Pamela Purifoy, who owns her own marketing firm called Purifoy Communications. Her company specializes in advertising, public relations, and promotions.*

**Rodney Hood talks with Pam Purifoy about one of her recent business promotions. They talk often and share information, ideas, and contacts.**

LJ:     Rodney, what is your role at the bank?

Rodney: I am responsible for finding ways in which our bank can stimulate economic growth and development in Raleigh, Durham, and Chapel Hill. We do that on a number of fronts. One is working with small businesses, to make sure that they have access to capital [money], so that they can operate vital, striving businesses. Another component is to promote affordable housing. I meet with builders, developers, and contractors to make sure that they have the resources they need to build multi-family or single-family housing.

Another part of my job is to meet with elected officials. I meet with the mayor, the city council, the county commissioners, and I try to get their ideas as to ways that our bank can help our community grow and prosper.

I also work with nonprofit organizations such as the hospitals, museums, schools, and daycare facilities. Our bank wants to make sure that those organizations have good active governing boards. If it will be helpful, for example, we will see if any of our employees can sit on those boards. We also see if the bank can make contributions to, say, special events, or that kind of thing.

So a lot of what I do basically boils down to me taking our bank out to the communities that we serve and trying to see what we can do to make an impact.

LJ:     What do you like about your job?

Rodney: I like the fact that I get to meet many people everyday. I meet probably five new people every day of the week. I like that because I get to talk to them about the bank and let them see the things that we can do.

I like the diversity of what I do. I get to do affordable housing one day, or one hour, and the next minute I can focus on a small business; then I can focus on the government aspects of finance. I constantly have to juggle five or six different projects. I like that, it makes the job challenging. Those are the things I enjoy the most.

## Activities for Developing Leadership Skills by Peggy Smith

1. Join a club like 4-H or Scouts. Or join a club at school like chess, photography, or Spanish. Once you have become acquainted with the people in the club, participate as fully as you have time. Offer to help out with the club activities. As you gain in experience, help out as an officer, coordinator, or chairperson. If your school can not find sponsors, ask a senior citizen or retired teacher to help with organization and chaperoning.

2. Volunteer for community service. Many organizations would love to have your help: schools, churches, nursing homes, hospitals, day care centers, animal shelters, and parks. Volunteer work is a great way to build people skills, and you will have the satisfaction of knowing that you are really doing something important.

3. Tutor someone your own age or a younger child. Share your skills with someone else. Your skills relate to school subjects like math or spelling, or another subject like playing the guitar, using a computer software program or game, amateur radio, baseball, or writing poetry. Giving something of yourself to another person is special.

4. Become a bus monitor or join your school's safety patrol. Talk to your school's guidance counselor about support groups for crisis intervention and prevention.

**5.** Become part of an artistic production; join a chorus, band, orchestra, dance group, or a theater production. Start a critical viewing/listening workshop for TV programs, music, and videos.

**6.** Ropes courses are fun and challenging. You learn a lot about teamwork, leadership, and risk-taking. They build inner strength and trust. A similar program is called Outward Bound. Ask your school counselor or physical education teacher if there are programs like this one in your area.

**7.** Look for meaningful work. Bring in the groceries when your parents bring them home. What work do the elderly people (e.g., neighbors or grandparents) in your life need? Yard work? Painting? Help clean up streams, parks, and beaches with groups like the Nature Conservancy or Sierra Club. Does your community have a Habitat for Humanity group? Call them up and see how you can help. Any fund drives for a good cause can teach phone skills. Be careful to go only to familiar and safe doors when soliciting face-to-face.

**8.** Any sport offers opportunities to develop leadership. Cooperation and teamwork, as well as goal-setting and shared fun, create lasting bonds among team sport participants. Leadership skills will be tested in both victory and defeat.

**Peggy Smith** is a firm believer in young adolescents. She supports fully their efforts to discover who they are and who they wish to become. Her favorite life experiences have been those as a parent, guardian, teacher, and administrator of young adolescents. Their energy, curiosity, intensity, passionate commitments to causes, and yes, even their pain, confusion, and disappointments, are all cause for her to celebrate her involvement with this age group. Her doctorate, earned at North Carolina State University, is in middle grades education.

## TEAMWORK SKILLS

In your future work, you are likely to work as a member of a team. Therefore, you need the following skills:

1. Work cooperatively with others; contribute to the group with ideas and effort.

2. Do your own share of tasks necessary to complete a project.

3. Encourage team members by listening to them, providing support, and offering tips for success, as appropriate.

4. Resolve differences for the benefit of the team.

5. Responsibly challenge existing procedures, policies, or authorities.

I asked Ozella Bland, lead teacher at a child care center, how important teamwork is in her job.

Ozella Bland's enthusiastic and friendly manner is appreciated by the children, parents, and the teachers with whom she works.

Ozella: It is very important. You must be able to get along with the people in the classroom. You need to be able to work together without using a lot of words. You need to be able to know what is going to happen. The way you do that is by getting to know the person who is with you. Hopefully, you two are on the same wavelength, defining discipline in the same way. You talk about what you like and what you want to accomplish in the classroom during your meeting times, so that when you come back to the classroom you can work together and accomplish those goals.

The more the children see you working together, the more they're going to work together. We stress a lot of sharing and cooperative play. You definitely want them to see that modeled by the adults. They learn by observing. They see everything you do. This age group picks up on things quickly and easily. They know right away if you are together. They know if there is any animosity; the children pick it up easily. So it is important to talk about what you want and work as a team.

Here is an example of how teamwork skills are used in a different setting—a manufacturing plant.

FACILITATOR FOR PRODUCTION MANUFACTURING. *This is a new job title for Nancy Bright. At Exide Electronics she used to be known as a production supervisor. When she had that title her job was to order people around, to tell them what to do. Now, she is a "facilitator." She helps the workers in her department work together as teams. Together, they build electric power systems. One of her teams—Larry Dorsey Moore, Barry Young, and Angelica Paparella—is shown below.*

99

Nancy Bright talks with the team about the quality of their work. She helps them work as a team.

LJ:      How do the teams work?

Nancy:  People who work as a team have their goals. They know their production schedule. It's up on this board [see photo]. This schedule is all I give them to get the
product out. I give them the information, and tell them what we need done, and
then they basically work out all the details on how to do it. And they do that as a
team.

Teamwork has made my job a lot easier because I don't have to make all the decisions. It also cuts down on a lot of overtime [when people work more than eight
hours in a day] because they team up to get things out. I don't need to go around
asking, "Can you work overtime?" They just help one another to get the work done
without overtime.

LJ:      So you see teamwork as an effective way for people to work?

Nancy:  Oh, definitely.

LJ:      Is it a plus for the people in the team?

Nancy:  There is always some adversity in anything you do like that, because you have different personalities. And when you first start something like this, you have to learn
how to do it. But we did a lot of team-building exercises. We did personality type
games, played games to learn what the different personalities are so people could
learn about one another. That helped a lot.

But like any other place, you don't always see eye to eye. We still have some negative times. If people have confrontations with associates, I let them go away and
handle it. I may stay outside the room at times, but I let them go inside a room and
talk it out. That way it wasn't me telling them what they have to do. And when
they come out of the room they are usually happy.

LJ:    Can you give an example of how a team has solved a problem?

Nancy:  Quality is always something we are trying to improve, and probably one of the biggest problems we work on around here is wiring errors. As a team, we think of all the causes, brainstorm on what causes us to have wiring errors, and work out a better way to do the wiring. As a team, we also work on raising the quality of our work, reducing costs, and improving the product.

## Activities for Developing Your Teamwork Skills by Penny Vagle

**1.** With two or three friends or classmates, set up a program to teach board games, or card games, to people in your class or younger children in your school or community. To do this, begin by surveying your class or friends to find out what card and board games they know (e.g., MONOPOLY, LIFE, chess, checkers, dominoes), who would be willing to teach these games, and who would like to learn different games. Based on your survey, set up learning centers. Each learning center needs a game, "teacher," and directions. Everyone can pick their own center to learn rules, directions, and game-playing strategies. You could do the same thing with computer programs, computer games, and major sports.

**2.** Volunteer to be a "buddy" to a younger child, a child with disabilities, or a new student in your school. Sit down with that person and find out what they like to do and what they need. Together, make a list of things to do or things that are needed. Together, prioritize your list (what to do first, second, third, etc.). Together, plan each activity and then carry them out together.

**3.** Volunteer with a friend to make an oral presentation in a class instead of turning in a written report. Make sure that you and your partner understand what is expected (e.g., topic, time limits of the presentation, location of the presentation). Brainstorm ideas related to the presentation. Write down *all* the ideas you think of. Evaluate your ideas. Discard any that do not fit. Map out your presentation. Decide what is needed to make your presentation (e.g., illustrations, props, charts). Divide the work load. Prepare the report. Practice the presentation with your partner and then give the presentation.

**4.** Volunteer to help a younger child with disabilities participate in Special Olympics. Be sure you know the rules of the sport and the adaptations needed by your child. Work out a schedule with the others involved in the activities. Know what's expected of you as a team member. Encourage your child, and be there when expected.

**5.** With your brother, sister, or friends, plan a family or neighborhood picnic. This involves planning activities to do, where to do them, and the food. Plan the day, time, and location. Consult first with everyone involved. Plan out any games you will play and any other activities. Plan what you will eat. Set up a budget. Decide who is responsible for what and when it should be done. Check with everyone to make sure tasks are being done in a timely manner. "Facilitate" at the picnic. Make sure everyone is involved and having a good time.

**6.** Instead of waiting for your parent(s) to organize household chores, you do it! Talk with the other members of your family. Identify weekly chores that need to be done and set up a schedule to see that everything gets done. Rotate the schedule weekly so that everyone gets their fair share of the "worst" jobs.

**7.** Volunteer in your community. Here are some ideas: join a reading program for younger children at your public library, be an assistant coach for Little League or other organized sports activity for younger children, help in a community clean-up effort, assist with recycling, or be an "assistant" in one of the summer programs offered by your Parks and Recreation Department or local school system.

**8.** With several other friends, organize a business. Some ideas include baby-sitting, dog walking, bringing in mail/newspapers for neighbors on vacation, or doing yard work or car washing. You'll need to plan together in the following areas: advertising, budgeting, scheduling jobs, hiring others to work for you, and payment (customers paying you and payments to you and your employees).

**9.** There are many opportunities for teamwork at school. Check out the following possibilities: run for student government or club office, work on the school newspaper or yearbook staff, be an office assistant, participate in junior varsity or intramural sports, organize a peer tutoring program (this could also be expanded to a nearby elementary school), participate in any job training opportunities arranged between your school and a local business, become a peer mediator, organize a new club, or participate in service clubs or in summer leadership training programs.

**Penny Vagle** works with the Wake County Public School System in Raleigh, North Carolina, as a program specialist in special education services. Part of her job includes work in the area of transition services—helping students prepare for what they'll be doing after they exit school (college, work, technical programs, etc.). Teamwork between student, family, school, and community agencies is required to do this.

## CULTURAL DIVERSITY SKILLS

You are an immigrant or you came from ancestors who were. Our country is a land of immigrants. All of us, or our ancestors, came from somewhere else. Consequently, we differ from each other in physical appearance and in cultural and ethnic backgrounds. This rich diversity in language, beliefs, and customs can be a plus or a minus. It can be the source of prejudice and hatred, or it can be the foundation of greatness.

Our diversity gives us many opportunities. In this country, you can be with, appreciate, learn from, and make friends with people who come from Nigeria, Cambodia, Japan, India, China, Egypt, Sweden, Iran, Russia, or many other countries, as well as with Native Americans. You can develop cultural diversity skills. These skills give you an advantage because the company you work for will likely sell its goods or services to other countries. You will know how to work with the diverse people from these countries in an effective, sensitive way. Imagine how much harder it would be if you grew up in country like Japan where virtually everyone is of Japanese descent!

Today's problems are complex, and as someone who values diversity, you are advantaged in problem solving. You are open and respectful of new ideas and different ways of doing things. You are better able to offer creative solutions. In addition, since most of today's problem solving is done by teams of people with diverse backgrounds, you are able to work effectively with them.

Furthermore, you will work with people of diverse backgrounds: customers, co-workers, and supervisors. Thus, you need skills to

1. work well with people having different ethnic, social, or educational backgrounds.

2. understand the concerns of members of other ethnic and gender groups.

3. base impressions on an individual's behavior not on stereotypes.

4. understand one's own culture and those of others and how they differ.

5. respect the rights of others while helping them make cultural adjustments where necessary.

Below are examples of how these skills are used in the workplace.

**CHILD CARE CENTER DIRECTOR.** *Rebecca Bowman's job as director of a child care center is described in Chapter 6, under "Speaking Skills." Rebecca is a good example of someone who frequently uses her cultural diversity skills. Her teachers and the parents come from a variety of racial and ethnic backgrounds. She uses all the skills listed above. In the photo below she is talking with one of her teachers, Edna Pableo.*

Rebecca Bowman listens to Edna Pableo, one of the teachers at the child care center.

**SCIENCE TEACHER, MIDDLE SCHOOL.** *Gregory Morris teaches students from a variety of backgrounds. His school has the English as a Second Language program for middle school students, so students who have just come to our country and do not know English come to his school. He works with many students whose knowledge of English is limited. Gregory is skilled at making them comfortable and helping them understand. The photo below shows him helping two students Vanessa Villalobos and Diego Soria, do a physics experiment.*

Gregory Morris is skilled in helping students from different backgrounds understand science.

Here is another example of cultural diversity skills.

**LICENSED PRACTICAL NURSE.** *The LPN helps patients who do not speak English communicate. The nurse tries to give or obtain information with gestures or tries to find another nurse who speaks the patient's language or arranges for an interpreter.*

## Activities for Developing Cultural Diversity Skills by LaVerne Weldon

**1.** With one or more partners (friends or family members), play a word association game. Choose a term from the list below for each round. In one minute, you and your partner(s) write down all other terms from this list that you associate with the chosen term and anything and everything that comes to your mind when you think of that term. After each round, discuss with each other why you wrote down what you did, and what influences your attitude and thinking about the terms.

| | | |
|---|---|---|
| Asian American | male | unemployed person |
| African American | female | employed person |
| Hispanic | rich person | nonprofessional |
| Caucasian | poor person | professional |

| Native American | middle-class person | elderly person |
| biracial | homemaker | fire fighter |
| supervisor | homosexual | high school dropout |
| handicapped person | college graduate | doctor |
| lawyer | teacher | engineer |
| nurse | printer | |

In doing this exercise, you identified your *stereotypes*. Your stereotypes are the *beliefs* you have *about classes or groups of people*. These beliefs can be positive or negative. Everyone has them. Unfortunately, they often mislead us. They can be harmful. For example, not long ago people believed that occupations like airplane pilot, scientist, and police officer were occupations that could only be done by men. Today, we know that is untrue, but this stereotype kept women from entering these occupations, women who would have really enjoyed these jobs. In addition, when women did begin to enter these jobs, they were often discriminated against. Racism and sexism are rooted in negative stereotypes. Consequently, it is very important that you and I be vigilant. We need to be aware of our stereotypes and not let these beliefs harm others or our relationships with them. (For more on stereotypes, see Chapter 12.)

**2.** Strike up a conversation with someone different from you, perhaps a person from the above list. Later, write down what interesting things you discovered about this person, and whether what you discovered agreed or disagreed with what you thought about the person before your conversation. Write a brief description about your discoveries.

**3.** While viewing a television show, movie, or newscast; reading or listening to a conversation; or speaking yourself, note at least three things that are said or seen about an individual or group of individuals that support a stereotype. Note anything that is said or seen that disproves a stereotype.

**4.** Say to yourself that for a period of time (for instance, a day) you will treat everybody the same regardless of their differences. Write about who you treated differently, and how and why you treated this person differently.

**5.** Read a magazine from another culture or ethnic group. Write about what you felt about what you read or saw.

**6.** Turn to a different kind of radio station (heavy metal, rock, jazz, rhythm and blues, country and western, classical, all news, religious) from the kind you normally listen to. Describe the kind of people you think normally listen to this station. Make a list of these kinds of people.

**7.** When someone in your presence is talking negatively or falsely about an individual or group of people, what do you do? Do you ever engage in this type of conversation? Do you ever correct someone who may be saying false or negative things about a person or group of people?  Make up a short skit about how you intervened on behalf of someone who was being portrayed negatively or falsely in a conversation.  You may choose to role play the scene.

**8.** Find out at least five facts about historical contributions of individuals from a racial or ethnic group other than your own.

**9.** Go to a restaurant and order food from a different ethnic group.  Find out at least three things about that culture.

**10.** Are all stereotypes negative?  List some positive stereotypes about a group of people.

**LaVerne Weldon** is an educator who finds great joy in what she does.  She graduated from Oberlin College with a B.A. degree in communications and for several years she taught seventh grade English in Philadelphia.  She earned her Master's degree in educational media at Temple University.  Presently LaVerne teaches English at St. Augustine's College in Raleigh, North Carolina, and is a doctoral student in education at North Carolina State University.  Recently, LaVerne designed and now teaches a course for middle school students in language arts.

## THINGS YOU CAN DO

Be sure to estimate your people skills on the next page.  Use your ratings to decide which skills you need to work on.  If you have read over the activities in this chapter, you know that there are a lot of great ones to choose from.  Choose the activities for the skills you need to strengthen.

## MY SELF-ESTIMATES FOR THE PEOPLE SKILLS

NAME _____

DATE _____

Rate yourself for each of the skills listed below. Compare yourself with other persons your age. Be sure to read the description of the skill if you are unsure what it means. Circle the appropriate number and *avoid rating yourself the same on each skill.*

**SOCIAL:** Show understanding, friendliness, and respect for feelings of others; assert oneself when appropriate; take an interest in what people say and why they think and act as they do.

HIGH   8   7   6   5   4   3   2   1   LOW

**NEGOTIATION:** Identify common goals among different parties; clearly present your position; understand other party's position; examine possible options; make reasonable compromises.

HIGH   8   7   6   5   4   3   2   1   LOW

**LEADERSHIP:** Communicate thoughts and feelings to justify a position; encourage or convince others; make positive use of rules or values; exhibit ability to have others believe in and trust you due to your competence and honesty.

HIGH   8   7   6   5   4   3   2   1   LOW

**TEAMWORK:** Contribute to group with ideas and effort; do own share of work; encourage team members; resolve differences for benefit of the team; responsibly challenge existing procedures, policies, or authorities.

HIGH   8   7   6   5   4   3   2   1   LOW

**CULTURAL DIVERSITY:** Work well with people having different ethnic, social, or educational backgrounds; understand the cultural differences of different groups; help people in these groups make cultural adjustments when necessary.

HIGH   8   7   6   5   4   3   2   1   LOW

# CHAPTER 9

# Personal Qualities

**W**hat do you do when you feel low? When things are just not going right? When you feel confused about where you are headed? Or, when you know that you have not handled a job well? These are common human feelings; everyone experiences them at one time or another. But did you know that you can learn skills that will minimize these negative feelings? Yes. If you learn and use these skills, you will experience negative feelings less often. And, you will be able to overcome them more easily when they do occur. These skills will make you a happier person. You will learn about these skills in this chapter.

## SELF-ESTEEM SKILLS

What can be more important than how we feel about ourselves? This section will go a long way toward explaining what affects your self-esteem. It will show you the basic steps toward having positive self-esteem. But, you will have to really pay attention. You will want to reread this section, and it is a good idea to discuss it with someone who understands these ideas. I can tell you that tens of thousands of people have benefited from understanding and applying these ideas, including myself and my family.

Did you know that low self-esteem can affect the occupation you choose? It's a fact. People with low self-esteem are less likely to choose an occupation that fits their abilities. For example, someone with low self-esteem may choose to be a nurse's aide even though they have the ability and desire to be a nurse or a doctor.

Low self-esteem can also negatively affect your work performance. I am sure you have seen this at school, or maybe in yourself. When people are "down," they are less motivated to work. They often have trouble concentrating, and the quality of their work suffers. Low self-esteem can have a negative effect on their relationships with other people. Sometimes they turn to drinking or taking drugs. More serious cases require the attention of a professional mental health specialist, like a counselor or a psychiatrist.

Your beliefs control how you feel. As William Shakespeare wrote long ago, "There is nothing either good or bad but thinking makes it so." This simple but powerful idea explains why your self-esteem is positive or negative. Everyone needs to learn this important lesson. To illustrate this, I would like you to think about the difficulties of teaching. As with all workers, teachers have setbacks and disappointments. Let's see how a teacher handles such a situation and how it affects her self-esteem.

Imagine Pat, a social studies teacher. This is her second year of teaching. She is always working to make her lessons interesting to students. This day, she is trying something different. She developed a new learning activity for students that she thinks they will enjoy and find helpful in learning about the United States Constitution. When she tries it out, the students find it confusing and frustrating. Pat is disappointed but not critical of herself. Instead of thinking, "Why can't I do things right? Why didn't I see that this was not going to work?," Pat thinks, "Well, I'm disappointed, but I will learn from this and try something different next time."

Let's take a close look at what happened to Pat by using the **A-B-C Approach.** We will first identify **A**, then **B**, and, finally, **C**:

**A** What was the *Activating event*? What started this experience? What happened? We can describe it this way: Pat tried out a new learning activity that confused and frustrated her students.

**B** What *Beliefs* did Pat have about A, what happened (i.e., the activating event)? She believed that "It will go better next time. It's not the end of the world."

**C** What were the *Consequences* of her belief about what happened? She felt disappointed and she was willing to try something different another time.

Do you see how her belief affected how she felt?

Now, imagine Pat had a *different belief* about what happened: "I must be perfect and I should never make people unhappy with me." How would this belief have affected how she felt about what happened? How she felt about herself? Her self-esteem? She would have felt deeply frustrated, discouraged, and disappointed with herself. Her self-esteem would have dropped. She might have decided not to try anything new in her classes.

In the next figure you can see this process illustrated. In the top part you can see how Pat reacted. In the bottom part you can see what would have happened if she had held irrational or harmful beliefs. Notice how such beliefs would lower her self-esteem.

| A | B | C |
|---|---|---|
| Activating Event | Her Beliefs | Consequences: Feelings & Behavior |
| Pat tried out new activity that confused and frustrated students. | I will do better next time. It's not the end of the world. | Disappointment. Will try a new activity later. **Keeps her positive self-esteem.** |
| *The outcome if she had had irrational or harmful beliefs:* | | |
| Pat tries out new activity that confuses and frustrates students. | This is terrible. I must be perfect. I should never make people unhappy with me. | Deeply frustrated and discouraged. Disappointed in herself. Does not try another new activity. **Low self-esteem.** |

From this example, you can see how our beliefs affect (a) how we feel and (b) what we do. To borrow from Shakespeare, the failure of the new class activity was not good or bad, it was "thinking that made it so." It was not the event itself, it was Pat's belief about the event that affected how she felt and what she did.

A number of common beliefs cause low self-esteem. Below are five examples of these irrational and harmful beliefs.

1. I am a *bad, unlovable person* if someone rejects me.

2. I am a *bad or worthless person* when I act weakly or stupidly.

3. I *must* be approved or accepted by people I find important!

4. *I can't stand* really bad things or very difficult people!

5. I *must do well* in everything I do or it is *terrible*.

(From A. Ellis, 1992, in L.K. Jones, *Encyclopedia of Career Change and Work Issues*, pp. 242-246, The Oryx Press.)

The specific self-esteem skills you want to learn and practice are

1. understanding how beliefs affect how a person feels and acts.

2. listening to what you say to yourself to identify any irrational or harmful beliefs you may have.

3. understanding how to change these negative beliefs when they occur.

Let's look at two other examples of how self-esteem skills are used in the workplace.

**OFFICE MANAGER.** *The office manager keeps a positive outlook when learning a new computer program for doing work in the office. When making mistakes in learning the program, the manager does not get discouraged and angry, thinking, "How can I be so stupid. I'll never learn* *this. They will find out and fire me."* Instead, the manager thinks, *"This is a challenge. I can learn these new skills with time. It is only natural to make mistakes when learning something new."* Can you analyze this office manager's experience using the A-B-C Approach? Can you imagine how this manager would have felt and acted if he held the belief, "I must do well in everything I do or it is terrible."? How would this belief have affected his self-esteem?*

Now let's talk to a real person, Jenny Joyner. She is the personnel manager at our local bank. She has a positive and intelligent approach to self-esteem.

Jenny Joyner keeps a positive outlook despite the disappointments that occur in her job.

LJ:     How important is your ability to manage your self-esteem?

Jenny:  Critical. You are dealing with people all the time in your job—the public or managers or your peers in your office. If you can't keep a positive attitude about yourself and life, then you can't remain objective about what you are doing. If you are on an even keel, then others are more likely to see you as reliable.

That's not to say that you don't feel low on some days about decisions you make. Such feelings are natural. But you have to be a self-motivator; you have to kick yourself in the rear and say "Okay, that's behind us, let's go on."

LJ:     Can you think of ways of keeping yourself up?

Jenny:  Talk to yourself a lot. You have to keep the person that you are in focus. Remember the good things that you have done and the things that you do well. Keep your perspective. Be positive and realistic in your thinking.

*"Most folks are about as happy as they make up their minds to be."*

— Abraham Lincoln

You will recall reading my interview with James Benton earlier (p. 18). He is a guest server's representative with Holiday Inn International who cannot see. He has been blind since birth, and has faced many disappointments. He says: "So many of us, when we get going each day, look for little things to agitate us, to complain about. There is too much good out here to focus on to worry about little things that may make you upset or miserable."

As you can see, James has a positive and realistic outlook on life. He believes in himself; he accepts who he is; he is proud of himself. And, even though he has had many disappointments in life, he has not let them get him down because he has realistic beliefs about life. Beliefs. They are the key.

## Activities to Develop Your Self-Esteem Skills by Angie Stephenson

**1.** We all have something that we can do really well. Whether it be changing a bicycle tire, diving off the high dive, baking chocolate chip cookies, or being a good listener to a friend. We all have special qualities. Usually bragging is something that most of us don't like to hear and we feel especially self-conscious when we say good things about ourselves, but as the saying goes—"Everything in moderation." For this exercise, freewrite for 10-15 minutes on the topic of bragging about the things that you think you do really well. Remember, I have given you suggestions and I know you can come up with a lot more about yourself. Start writing and don't stop until you have at least one page.

**2.** Using the freewrite that you created in the first activity, create a visual advertisement that brags about three of your special qualities. You should use colorful images and creative ideas to share with your classmates the things you can do well. Try to make the shape of your collage symbolic as well. For example, I might make a visual in the shape of a cookie with a couple of chips to represent your special qualities. You can expect your classmates to giggle a bit; after all it isn't everyday that we can brag about ourselves.

**3.** During several days keep a running log of what you hear people say about themselves. You can focus on a couple of people or many different people, such as friends, family members, teachers, and strangers with whom you have daily contact. After collecting these comments, analyze your findings. You can get as statistical as you want to and visual representations may be helpful—use bar graphs to show the number of people who say positive or negative things about themselves. Finally, write a brief reaction to your findings and discuss how these statements can reflect self-esteem and the effect that the statements may have on their speakers.

**4.** Interview a family member or other adult about his or her life at your age. Ask your interviewee to be as honest as possible about how he or she saw him or herself when younger, and then, after discussing this question at length, ask the person to reflect on how those times shaped the person he or she has become. You should develop a list of 7-10 questions in relation to the topic. For example: What was your biggest weakness and how did you deal with it? If you could have changed one physical trait, what would it have been and why? How do you feel about that trait today? After the interview, draw all your information together into a profile of the individual. At the end of the profile, include your reactions to what you learned as well as any similarities that you might possess in your own life.

**5.** Create a personal crest in the spirit of a family shield or coat-of-arms that represents accomplishments you have made in your life. Your crest should be colorful and symbolic and should contain one positive adjective that you think best describes you. Check with family members if you have a hard time thinking of things to include. Often, we don't recognize our many accomplishments, but others certainly do!

**6.** With a small group of classmates, brainstorm quotes of encouragement that you could share with others. Your quotes can be researched or original, or perhaps a combination of both. After coming up with 5-7 quotes, create colorful strips that you can post about the room. You might also make individual-sized reproductions of your quotes so that you can give them to others at a time when they especially need some encouragement—right before a test or right before a big dance, for example.

**7** Create a GIG folder—"Gosh, I'm Great!" You should decorate this in a way to remind you of all the wonderful, positive things that make you special and unique. Then, on a day determined by the class, you will have "GIG Note Day" where each student will write something positive to every other student in the class. You might consider ideas such as, "You have a wonderful smile and you make me smile when I come into the classroom." or "Your great sense of humor really makes this class more fun!" All comments should be positive and you might even choose to remind your classmates of some of your previous quotes of encouragement. As a class or individually, you can determine when to read these GIG notes. Perhaps you'd like to do one at the start of every other day or maybe you'd rather read them when you aren't feeling too good about things. Either way, GIG Notes are sure to be fun for everyone.

**8.** With your teacher's help, choose a book of Young Adult literature that deals with a theme associated with developing self-esteem. After reading the text, write a brief response in which you discuss the major conflicts facing the main character and how she or he confronts and resolves them.

**9.** Make someone feel good about him or herself today and you too will feel better about yourself. Smile!

**Angie Stephenson** teaches at Leesville Road High School in the English Department. She has been a teacher for eight years and has always enjoyed teaching as well as learning. Angie has received two undergraduate degrees and will receive her Master's degree in May 1995. On self-esteem, Angie writes: "I find self-esteem to be the most important part of being. Without positive self-esteem, it is impossible to truly achieve our potential. When we feel poorly about ourselves, others respond the same way toward us. When we project good feelings about ourselves, we attract more good feelings."

## Activities that Use the "A-B-C Approach"

Many students have found these activities helpful. So have I. I highly recommend them to you.

**1.** *Keep a thought log.* It can help you see how your beliefs (**B**) about events (**A**) affect your feelings and behavior (**C**). Take a loose-leaf paper and make three vertical columns. First, in the left-hand column, briefly describe the activating event (**A**) that occurred just before you experienced the strong emotions. Second, in the far right column, write down what we called the consequences (**C**): the emotions you felt, and what you did, like crying or running away. Then, in the middle column, write down the beliefs (**B**) you had about what happened, about the "activating event."

Write in your thought log whenever you feel strong emotions. You may want to do it at meal times. Once you get the hang of it, you will see how your beliefs affect your feelings and behavior. The thought log is particularly useful if you have low self-esteem. You will identify your negative self-talk, the irrational harmful beliefs that make you suffer. Ask yourself, "Do I have any of the irrational harmful beliefs mentioned earlier in this section (p. 110)? If you do, you will find the following activities helpful.

**On the next page is a thought log form that you can photocopy and use.**

**2.** Exercise aerobically on a regular basis, at least several times a week. This is especially helpful if you frequently experience strong emotions like stress, anger, or anxiety.

**3.** Argue against your irrational thoughts. Pick apart their faulty logic. For example, it is irrational for you to get down on yourself because you make a mistake. It's irrational to believe that you must be perfect. No one is. It's impossible to be perfect. If you see this "perfectionist" belief appearing in your thought log, jump on it. Dispute it. Say why it is illogical. Tell yourself, "This is irrational!" To learn more about irrational thoughts and why they are irrational or harmful, read one of the good books listed below:

Lawrence Jones. (1992). *Encyclopedia of Career Change & Work Issues.* Phoenix: The Oryx Press (see the articles on "Self-Talk" and "Rational Thinking").

David Burns. (1980). *Feeling Good.* New York: New American Library.

Albert Ellis. (1988). *How to Stubbornly Refuse to Make Yourself Miserable About Anything—Yes, Anything!* Secaucus, NJ: Lyle Stuart.

**4.** Try "thought stopping and substitution." When you notice that your self-talk is negative, you yell (either out loud or quietly depending on where you are) "STOP!" Then substitute a rational thought for the negative one. For example, let's say that you have a disagreement with a friend, and she tells you that she dislikes you and doesn't want to see you anymore. Later, you find yourself talking negatively to yourself, "How could I have said that to her? I was so stupid.

# THOUGHT LOG

| **A** | **B** | **C** |
|---|---|---|
| Activating Event | My Beliefs about the Activating Event | Consequences: Feelings & Behavior |

What a jerk I am. This is really terrible! She was one of my best friends." To which you would yell, "STOP!" and say to yourself, "I made a mistake, but I'm human. I will apologize to her. If she refuses to accept my apology, I will be disappointed. I will miss being her friend, but I will make other friends."

**5.** Say, "Yes!" to yourself. Write positive self-talk statements about your abilities and qualities. For example, "I am improving my keyboarding skills by practicing on the computer each day." When you write your statements, be sure they are accurate. Don't say something about yourself that you don't really believe. Also, avoid making statements that are broad and general like, "I'm a good person." Be specific like the example I gave above. Write eight to ten of these positive statements about yourself on an index card and read them out loud two times a day. Some people like to record them on a tape recorder and play them back.

**6.** If you have persistent feelings of low self-esteem, talk with your parents about getting help. Talk with your school counselor. With hard work, you can overcome these negative feelings. There is no need to suffer.

## SELF-MANAGEMENT SKILLS

In today's world, it is important to learn to manage yourself. You need to learn to manage your health (exercise and diet), time, job performance, and self-improvement.

You *must* have self-management skills to succeed in the workplace. Here are just a few examples of how these skills are used: handling job stress, learning new skills and knowledge, improving the quality of the work you do, learning how to express anger and other feelings appropriately, managing your time effectively, overcoming procrastination or perfectionism, and strengthening assertiveness.

Fortunately, psychologists have studied self-management and identified the skills you need to learn.

1. Assess your own knowledge and skills accurately.

2. Set well-defined and realistic personal goals.

3. Monitor your progress toward your goals.

In the leadership skills section of the last chapter, I interviewed Rodney Hood, a community investment coordinator at a local bank. Like all the working people I know, Rodney continues to strengthen and upgrade his skills for his job at the bank.

LJ:      What things do you do to strengthen your work skills?

Rodney: Because of this computer age, I am constantly going back and getting refresher courses on computer programs, like Windows. I go to a lot of workshops, such as developmental workshops on how to understand private and public organizations better. I am going to be at the University of North Carolina at Chapel Hill in three

Rodney Hood is continually strength-ening his skills.

weeks for a week's seminar on accounting. I take refresher courses on things I need to really know to be a good banker. I am constantly trying to fine tune my skills.

Another excellent example of self-management skills is shown by Jenny Joyner whom I interviewed earlier in this chapter (p. 111). She is the personnel manager for a large bank. Listen to what she says.

Jenny: I need to strengthen my speaking skills. I talk to groups of people and give pre-sentations on benefits and on other topics. Speaking skills are going to be even more important for me because we are getting ready to do benefits training. I am fairly new in my job, so improving my speaking skills is something that I am going to have to work on.

LJ: In the book, we talk about self-management skills. When you talk about strength-ening your speaking skills, that is exactly what I am talking about. What have you done to strengthen your speaking skills?

Jenny: I am lucky in that a good friend of mine is a speech communications Master's stu-dent at the University of North Carolina. I bought a book of hers called *Speech Communications*, and I am now reading through it. My husband is in business school, and we both have identified speaking skills as a weakness, so we are work-ing together on improving those skills. I try to identify the particular areas that I want to work on, and I hope I will benefit from that.

Another thing I do is think about what I did during the day on my long ride home to Chapel Hill every day after work. I think about what has gone well and what I could do to improve. I take the best from what I have done well and remember it, and I look at what didn't go so smoothly and remember that, and what I can do to improve. Remembering what didn't go well helps a lot; next time I may choose a different path or say a different thing.

Do you want to learn more about these self-management skills? Read and study the sections in Chapter 13 called "Short-Term Goals" and "Planning Skills." The tips in these sections will help you a great deal. They will also help you with the activities described below.

## Activities for Developing Self-Management Skills by Penny Vagle

**1.** Do an *information interview*. Talk with someone working in an occupation of interest to you to learn about their work. The interview is a terrific way to learn about an occupation and, later, to get a good job! To do the interview, follow the steps given below.

a. List five occupations that interest you. Research each job. Your school librarian or counselor can help you. Find out the following:

What kind of skills are needed for each job?

How much education is required?

What kind of courses would you need to take in high school? College? Technical school?

What is the salary range?

Is there room for advancement? What kind?

What job opportunities are there in this area?

b. Set a realistic goal, such as "I will work on doing an information interview for two hours a week until I have succeeded in following all the steps." Keep a record of the amount of time (minutes or quarter hours) you work on it, and reward yourself each week when you meet your goal.

c. Develop a list of whom you might contact. Get ideas from friends, family members, teachers, your school counselor, or the yellow pages in the telephone book.

d. Write down the questions you want to ask. Here are some good ones:

What do you do in a typical day?

What do you like most and least about your job?

What skills and abilities are important in your work?

How should a person prepare for entering this occupation?

What are the problems and frustrations you face in your job or organization?

What is the job outlook? Will there be many jobs in the future in this area?

Can you tell me the names of other people who do the same kind of work? Can I say that you suggested that I contact them?

e. Write a brief, personal letter to your contact person asking for an appointment. Briefly give the purpose of your interview (e.g., "I am thinking of going into your occupation and want to learn about it to see if it fits me.") and how long you expect it will last (e.g., "about 30 minutes"). Say that you will call for an appointment.

f. Call the person and restate your request and set up an appointment.

g. Do the interview. Be sure to get there in plenty of time and dress appropriately. Ask open-ended questions. Take notes occasionally of important points. Watch the clock and leave when your interview was scheduled to end.

h. Write the person a thank you note afterwards. This is very important. Be sure to do it.

i. Keep the person informed of your progress. Send a note to him or her later.

**2.** Identify a class that you are having trouble with at school. Keep a tally for three days on how many questions you ask in class and what they are. Also list questions asked by other students. On a sheet of paper make three columns. From left to right, label them: Who, Number of Questions, and Examples of Questions. On the night of the third day, study your tallies. Decide what types of questions get the most information (e.g., "What time is it?" versus "Would you please check this to see if I'm doing it correctly?"). Work on increasing the number of your own questions and the appropriateness of your questions. Set a goal for yourself. For example, "For each two-day period, I will ask at least one question in each class." Give yourself a few weeks and then for three days keep a record of your questions, as before. This way you will see if you are asking appropriate questions more often. Decide if you are asking the questions needed to get the information or assistance you need.

**3.** Learn how to negotiate when you're having a problem or conflict with a friend or adult. Read the section in Chapter 8 of this book on "Negotiation Skills" (pp. 91-94) and the activities you can do to strengthen these skills (pp. 93-94) and start doing them. Set a goal for yourself that you will use these skills the next time you are having a problem or conflict with someone. After the next conflict occurs, sit down and analyze how well you used these skills. Work on those skills that need to be strengthened.

**4.** Develop a budget so that you can plan to save for something you want. In developing a budget, answer the following questions:

What do I want to buy or do?

How much money will I need?

How much money do I get for an allowance or job—weekly or monthly?

What is my spending pattern? For at least three weeks, keep a tally of your spending by category. For example, the categories might be "Clothes," "Food/Snacks," and "Tapes/CDs." Decide where you want to stop "throwing money away." Eliminate that item from your budget or reduce spending in it. Then, set a weekly savings goal, "I will save $_____ each week." Each week put the money in the bank or give it to your parent(s) to keep for you.

**5.** Set a goal and achieve it. The following are examples of goals you might work on:

Get to school on time every day for two weeks.

Study _____ hours per week.

Exercise aerobically for at least 30 minutes four times a week.

Spend _____ hours per week practicing _____.

Spend _____ hours per week learning about occupations I am interested in.

Clean my room _____ times per week.

Spend _____ hours per week helping another person.

**Penny Vagle** works in the Wake County Public School System in Raleigh, North Carolina, as a program specialist in special education services. Part of her job includes work in the area of transition services—helping students prepare for what they'll be doing after they exit school (college, work, technical programs, etc.). According to Penny, "Students need to learn how to be actively involved in making the decisions that affect them. It's important to start learning this at an early age so that you'll be comfortable working with adults and agencies that will be important to you later in your life."

Be sure to read the sections in Chapter 13 on goal-setting and planning (pp. 161-164)!

## RESPONSIBILITY SKILLS

Companies frequently make statements like, "Quality is Job Number One." They know that in order to compete and succeed, their products and services must meet the highest standards. Would you buy a car that leaks when it rains? Or go to a bank where the teller is rude because she is bored? Of course not. Companies know that customers expect quality. Quality is the company's responsibility.

Similarly, you need responsibility skills. Are companies going to hire or keep you if you do poor quality work or are late to work? No. People need to know that they can depend on you. You need the following skills:

1. Give a high level of effort toward reaching goals.

2. Work hard to become excellent at job tasks. Pay attention to details. Concentrate at doing tasks well, even unpleasant ones.

3. Display high standards of attendance, honesty, energy, and optimism.

Here are two examples of how these skills are used in the workplace.

**COIL WINDER.** *Jonnie Bryant makes a coil for one Exide Electronics product. It is a vital part, and it must be built according to specifications. The specifications are given on a sheet that tells her such things as what parts to use, how many turns the copper wire needs to be wound around the core, and so on.*

Jonnie Bryant builds the coil according to specifications.

Even though this job may get boring at times, Jonnie always concentrates on her work to be sure it is done right and on time. She told me: "Quality is the number one thing as far as I am concerned. I hate having a part I make rejected."

**MEDIA SPECIALIST.** *Like all jobs, Bettie Dew's job as a media specialist has its boring and frustrating moments, but she works hard to do her best and keep a cheerful outlook. I was impressed with her enthusiasm in helping students. In the photo below, she is helping Thao Nguyen learn how to use the computer.*

**Bettie Dew enjoys helping students like Thao Nguyen learn to use the computer.**

## Activities for Developing Responsibility Skills by Candy Beal

Responsibility is a tricky thing. You can be a very responsible person and never have anyone tell you how responsible they think you are. Actions, however, speak louder than words. Those considered responsible are the first ones selected for a job or asked to handle a problem. Show you are responsible by being resourceful, patient, and dependable. It's important to arrive on time, take the job seriously, be positive, and stick with the job until it's done.

Everybody wants others to think they are responsible, but the real person who's important in this is you. If you know you've done your best, you can't second guess yourself. Sometimes you'll mess up. That's life. Making a mistake is one of the ways we learn. The trick is that you do learn and try not to let it happen again. That's being responsible.

There are many things you can do to develop responsibility. They may not be the paying jobs you'd like to have now, but they establish your track record and make it easier for you to get chances for other things. Don't kid yourself—jobs and responsibility aren't just about money. Volunteering pays big dividends in the way you feel about yourself. When you start thinking no one appreciates you, try volunteering. You'll learn just how valuable you really are!

**1.** Volunteer to help at the local hospital or clinic. Both males and females are welcome and the jobs are varied and interesting. The work will give you a great chance to learn about jobs in the medical profession. Much of what you do will require teamwork and you'll have the satisfaction of knowing you've helped complete a complex task. You'll be a good PR person for adolescents. The adults who run the volunteer office will see you as dependable, hospital staff will count on you to help them, and patients will see that teens can make valuable contributions.

**2.** Volunteer at your school. This can often be done during study hall, club day, or service club. Join your school's peer mediation program. If you don't have the time during school, why not consider something you can do after school or on the weekends? Grounds beautification or helping at the concession stand during a sports activity are some after-school options.

3. Has your school ever done the egg, five pounds of flour, or grapefruit "babies" project? If not, here's how it works. A teacher asks you to bring in one of the above items. You are responsible for caring for that item for one week. You treat it as you would a baby. It goes everywhere with you and needs your constant care. At the end of the week you'll know what it is to be truly responsible for the care of something. Sorry, but you can't hard boil the egg. You may also want to consider the rapid ripening of unrefrigerated grapefruit. I'd go with the sack of flour. Everyone could donate the flour to the Food Bank at the end of the week.

4. If your campus is near an elementary school, you can work with younger children as a reading or study buddy. In the spring, the fifth graders would appreciate a short course in "Moving Up to Middle School."

5. One of the most valuable things you can do in your school is to be a friend and helper to a physically challenged child. You can learn patience from them and by your show of support help to educate your friends to all that these children can do.

6. Is your school located near a day care center, YMCA/YWCA, or senior citizen's housing facility? An after-school project that gives you a chance to help at these places would be a good way to do community volunteering. Check with your guidance counselor and see if she or he can suggest a sponsor for the students who want to get involved. In the summer, churches are in need of help with their Vacation Bible School and Mother's Morning Out programs. The SPCA is always looking for help with kennel care.

7. Looking for jobs around your neighborhood might lead you to pet sitting, car washing, child care, and grass cutting. Use your powers of observation to identify neighbors who might no longer be able to keep up their house and yard chores. They would appreciate your helping hand.

8. Finally, don't overlook the best proving ground for responsibility—your own home. Set up a schedule for getting jobs done around the house. Not having to be asked will amaze your parents! Volunteering also goes a long way to showing you are responsible enough to handle more freedom, worthy of the cost of a movie or two, or of using the family car!

**Candy Beal** is a doctoral student at North Carolina State University studying and working with adolescents and schools. She learned the lesson of responsibility the hard way when she forgot to lay out her clothes the night before her first day of preschool. She grabbed anything, dressed in a hurry, and forgot to put on one key item. Back in the 1950s when little girls wore dresses and playground slides were metal, this was a real problem. I'm happy to say that she's been very responsible ever since and enjoys the opportunity to take on tasks that show people what a good job she can do.

## THINGS YOU CAN DO

Use the rating scale below to estimate your strengths in the personal quality skills. Photocopy it and rate yourself. Then, based on your ratings, do the activities in this chapter that will help you the most.

## MY SELF-ESTIMATES FOR THE PERSONAL QUALITIES SKILLS

NAME _____

DATE _____

Rate yourself for each of the skills listed below. Compare yourself with other persons your age. Be sure to read the description of the skill if you are unsure what it means. Circle the appropriate number and *avoid rating yourself the same on each skill.*

**SELF-ESTEEM:** Understand how beliefs affect how a person feels and acts; "listen" and identify irrational or harmful beliefs you may have; and understand how to change them when they occur.

HIGH 8 7 6 5 4 3 2 1 LOW

**SELF-MANAGEMENT:** Assess own knowledge and skills accurately; set specific, realistic personal goals; monitor progress toward goals.

HIGH 8 7 6 5 4 3 2 1 LOW

**RESPONSIBILITY:** Work hard to reach goals, even if task is unpleasant; do quality work; display high standard of attendance, honesty, energy, and optimism.

HIGH 8 7 6 5 4 3 2 1 LOW

PART

three

# SPECIAL SKILLS AND CAREER PLANNING

# Choosing Your Career Direction

xploring your career options will help you make good decisions. Having some idea of where you are headed, a career direction, will guide you in your decisions. For example, knowing that construction work is your career direction will point you toward certain occupations in the field: surveyor, civil engineer, project manager, carpenter, electrician, or heavy equipment operator. You can then learn about these occupations, what Special Skills they require, and how to prepare for them.

## CAREER EXPLORATION

There are many interesting and useful ways to learn about yourself and occupations. One way is to take a career interest inventory and see what occupations it suggests. You can do this in Chapter 5. In this section, we will look at several other ways you can explore your options.

### Volunteer Work

I recently met Roya Ardeshirpour, a junior at Leesville Road High School. She volunteered to tutor Franklin Swain, an elementary school student, in reading.

By tutoring Franklin Swain with his reading, Roya Ardeshirpour is getting a better idea of whether she wants a career working with children.

In addition to helping Franklin (and he really appreciates it), Roya is using this experience to explore her career interests. She explains, "I think I want to be a pediatrician [a doctor who works with children], so I wanted to see how it really felt working with children. So far, I've enjoyed it."

## Career Decision-Making Courses

Many schools have courses designed to help you explore and make decisions about careers. They can help you learn about yourself and occupations that might fit you. It also helps you make wise decisions and good educational and career plans. Why not see what your school offers?

## Courses Oriented to Problem Solving

Do you avoid math and science courses because they are too abstract and theoretical? Because they do not seem practical? Do you learn best when you can apply what you learn in class to practical, hands-on problems? Then you will be interested in a new breed of courses.

Most schools now offer challenging courses in science and math that are technically oriented. That means they are less abstract and more oriented toward problem solving. These are courses for people who want to enter occupations that offer good pay and are technical- or science-related. Many students like these courses because they can apply what they learn in class to real, practical problems. Plus, they learn skills that are in demand in the workplace.

An excellent example is the Applied Mathematics course taught at Cary High School by Michael Kelley. In this class, students often work in teams and learn valuable team-work skills. The students like that.

When I visited, they were learning the basic math concepts used in land surveying. They were in the front of the school learning about elevations and vertical angles.

Michael Kelley explains to his students how they can use a theodolite to solve the practical problems of surveying.

Terry McLean takes his turn at using the theodolite.

Find out what applied courses your school has in such areas as math, science, writing, computers, and technology.

## Informational Interview

Interview people in the work you are considering. This is a great way to really learn a lot. Most people are happy to talk about their work, and it can be very informative. Penny Vagle describes how to do this in Chapter 9 in the section entitled "Developing Self-Management Skills." I highly recommend this.

## Job Shadowing

In job shadowing, you actually "shadow" someone working in an occupation in which you are interested. It might be for a few hours, or a whole day. Ask your school counselor for ideas. Kai Cheng was able to do this through a program called "Youth-in-Business Day," which is sponsored by the City of Raleigh Parks and Recreation Department.

In the photo below, Kai is shadowing Sandra White, an engineering technician with Carolina Power and Light. She is explaining to Kai how she is able to communicate with 1,800 specially equipped power meters with her computer. With her computer, Sandra can "read" them the same way your meter reader does when he or she comes to look at it. These special meters are usually placed where it is unsafe for a meter reader to go, for example, a high crime area.

Kai Cheng listens to Sandra White explain what she does as an engineering technician.

Kai is a junior in high school. He is most interested in the field of electrical engineering. That is why he wanted to shadow Sandra. He is taking courses in electronics and computer science to prepare himself for this field.

## Computerized Career Guidance Systems

These systems are designed to help you identify occupations you should consider and to give you information about them. They are commonly found in school libraries or career centers. Ask your school counselor about them.

## Career Reference Books

There are a number of excellent books you can read to learn about occupations. I already mentioned the *Guide for Occupational Exploration* and its more recent version the *Complete Guide for Occupational Exploration*. Some of the many other good possibilities include:

*Occupational Outlook Handbook* (U.S. Department of Labor)

*Encyclopedia of Careers and Vocational Guidance* (Ferguson)

*Career Discovery Encyclopedia* (Ferguson)

*Career Guide to Industries* (U.S. Department of Labor)

## OCCUPATIONAL PROFILE

You will want to write down what you learn about occupations. To do this in an organized way, use the form I created on the next page. Photocopy it and then write in what you learn. Put each of these profiles in your Job Skills Portfolio (see Chapter 16).

## Occupational Profile

**Name of Occupation** _____

   **1.** Nature of the work (what the person does):

   **2.** Education, training, skills, and experience needed:

   **3.** Location where these persons work:

   **4.** Earnings (average salary or wages):

   **5.** Job outlook (number of job openings expected):

   **6.** Opportunities for advancement:

   **7.** Similar or related occupations:

   **8.** Advantages and disadvantages of this work:

## Summary

You have many opportunities. This is a good time to explore, to learn about yourself and the world about you. As you do this, you will develop a clearer career direction and get a better idea as to which skills you want to learn.

In the next chapter, we will look at your *motivated skills* and see how you can use them as a compass to point you in the right career direction.

# Your Motivated Skills

hoose something you enjoy doing." I heard this remark over and over again when I interviewed people for this book. I asked them, "What advice do you have for students who are choosing an occupation?" That's what they said—"Choose something you enjoy doing." And that is what this chapter is about: identifying the skills you particularly enjoy using—*your motivated skills.*

A good example of this is a student I met in our School of Design, Abelardo Dextré. That's his photo on the next page. Look at the happiness and pride on his face. Can there be any doubt about what his motivated skill is?

Abelardo Dextré is holding two designs he created.

The first design, in his right hand, he made in black and white. He followed this by creating the color design in his left hand. He then used this color design to create the "cityscape" in the next photo.

Abelardo's "cityscape" created from his earlier design.

Abelardo obviously loves design. This *motivated skill* is guiding his career direction. He is studying to become an architect.

In this book, you have met many people who use their motivated skills in their work: I think of Mitchell Ward (p. 66) and her skills of listening and helping people with their careers, and of Jorge Vasquez (p. 75) and his skills in genetics, problem solving, and math that he uses to save tropical pine forests.

Not everyone is so fortunate to be able to use their most loved skills in their work. Sometimes these skills are not that marketable. How many people can make a living singing, for example? An alternative is to use these skills outside of work in hobbies or volunteer activities.

Nevertheless, it is important to know what your motivated skills are. That way, you will know what to aim for. This knowledge can serve as a compass for your career direction. So, let's get started identifying them.

## IDENTIFYING YOUR MOTIVATED SKILLS

To begin, I want you to meet Summer Ibrahim. She discovered her motivated skills and is pleased with the result. To identify these skills, she used the Skills Inventory that you will find on pages 138-141.

Summer Ibrahim working on her Skills Inventory.

Summer enjoyed using her past achievements to learn what her motivated skills are. For example, one of her achievements was singing Christmas carols to the elderly at a nursing home. She did this with her youth group. When she examined the activities she did at the nursing home, she was able to identify the skills she used as the following:

- Performed before an audience

- Sang or played a musical instrument

- Responded with warmth and courtesy

- Understood people's feelings

- Worked with a team or group

- Empowered people, raised their self-esteem

- Helped the sick or injured

- Talked easily with all kinds of people

- Dealt with people with tact and courtesy

Summer enjoys using all these skills. Yes, these are her motivated skills! Now, she can use this knowledge to identify possible occupations. She can use it as a career compass. For example, these skills are used in such occupations as Music Teacher, Singer, Social Worker, Nurse, School Counselor, and Respiratory Therapist, to name a few.

## YOUR ACHIEVEMENTS

You will go through six steps to identify your motivated skills. This process will take time, at least an hour. So be sure to allow enough time. You will want to take a break midway. It will take patience and effort. But, at the end, you will know it was worth it. You will be pleased and proud of the result. You will know your job strengths.

It is best to do this with another person if you can, or a small group of three to four people. That way you can help each other. I will describe here how to do it by yourself and show you how to do it with a group in the section at the end of the chapter entitled, "Things You Can Do."

To make the steps clearer, we will follow Nathan Buescher, one of my student "editors" from Daniels Middle School.

**STEP ONE:** List the things that you have accomplished, achievements that you feel good about. Brainstorm about this. Freely think back through this past year, then the past several years, and write down 15 or 20 of your accomplishments. Don't be concerned about whether other people think they are important or not. What is important is how you feel. These achievements might have involved a club (like Boy or Girl Scouts, YWCA, or 4-H), church, school, work, hobby, family, sports, games, or something you did on your own. Write down whatever comes to mind. Take your time. Leave a space of about three lines between each achievement that you list.

**STEP TWO:** Write down a description of each achievement in the space you left below it. For each one, recall what happened and write down what you felt you *did* that made you feel good about the achievement.

After thinking about it, Nathan was able think of quite a few achievements.

Nathan wrote down, "Helped people build a house for Habitat for Humanity." I asked him for more details: "I went out to this place where they were building a house. There were all these bamboo canes in the yard, and we cleared a lot of that out."

**STEP THREE:** Review the achievements you listed and place a check mark (✓) next to the seven you feel have been most important to you.

**STEP FOUR:** Rank-order the seven achievements. Number them from one to seven. "Achievement #1" is the one you feel is most important to you; "Achievement #2" is second most important, and so on.

These are Nathan's seven achievements, rank-ordered:

1. In NJHS [National Junior Honor Society—requires a 3.5 grade point average for membership and allows members to take part in school and community service projects].

2. Helped people build a house for Habitat for Humanity.

3. Rafted down the French Broad River.

4. Helped sick family members.

5. Learned how to play the piano.

6. Performed in a play

7. Build a $CO_2$ car and won the race.

**STEP FIVE:** This step has two parts: (a) you write a detailed description of what you did in each achievement, and (b) identify the skills you used to accomplish each achievement by using the Skills Inventory on pages 138-141.

To begin, take out a blank piece of paper and at the top write a brief title for Achievement #1. Then, below it, describe what you did in this achievement. What were your activities? Did you play a musical instrument? Use particular tools? Write? Read? Use mathematics? Relate to people in a particular way (e.g., teach, persuade, organize them)? Don't give your reasons for doing these activities. Just write down what you did to make it happen.

Be sure to describe your achievement in enough detail so that you can identify the skills you used.

Now, take your description of Achievement #1 and identify the skills you used with the Skills Inventory (you will need to make a photocopy of it). At the top of the Skills Inventory, in the first column, write the title of your achievement. Then, go down that column and check the (✓) skills you used to do it. Repeat this process for the remaining six achievements.

When you look at the Skills Inventory, starting on the next page, you will see listed under "sample" the skills that Nathan checked for his first achievement, National Junior Honor Society.

Take your time in doing this step. It is very important. You may want to take a break along the way.

## SKILLS INVENTORY

Write your achievements in, then check off the skills you used in each one.

| Skills | sample | 1 | 2 | 3 | 4 | 5 | 6 | 7 |
|---|---|---|---|---|---|---|---|---|
| **REALISTIC SKILLS** | | | | | | | | |
| Trained animals | ___ | ___ | ___ | ___ | ___ | ___ | ___ | ___ |
| Raised animals or grew plants | ___ | ___ | ___ | ___ | ___ | ___ | ___ | ___ |
| Helped people in safety situations | ___ | ___ | ___ | ___ | ___ | ___ | ___ | ___ |
| Used higher level mathematics | ___ | ___ | ___ | ___ | ___ | ___ | ___ | ___ |
| Solved mechanical problems | ___ | ___ | ___ | ___ | ___ | ___ | ___ | ___ |
| Protected people or property | ___ | ___ | ___ | ___ | ___ | ___ | ___ | ___ |
| Maintained machines or equipment | ___ | ___ | ___ | ___ | ___ | ___ | ___ | ___ |
| Inspected objects | ___ | ___ | ___ | ___ | ___ | ___ | ___ | ___ |
| Navigated | ___ | ___ | ___ | ___ | ___ | ___ | ___ | ___ |
| Used hands skillfully | ___ | ___ | ___ | ___ | ___ | ___ | ___ | ___ |
| Operated machines used in construction | ___ | ___ | ___ | ___ | ___ | ___ | ___ | ___ |
| Measured or cut with precision | ___ | ___ | ___ | ___ | ___ | ___ | ___ | ___ |
| Handled construction hand tools | ___ | ___ | ___ | ___ | ___ | ___ | ___ | ___ |
| Used arithmetic or shop geometry | ___ | ___ | ___ | ___ | ___ | ___ | ___ | ___ |
| Studied blueprints or drawings | ___ | ___ | ___ | ___ | ___ | ___ | ___ | ___ |
| Operated precision instruments | ✓ | ___ | ___ | ___ | ___ | ___ | ___ | ___ |
| Repaired or adjusted something | ___ | ___ | ___ | ___ | ___ | ___ | ___ | ___ |
| Built or installed something | ___ | ___ | ___ | ___ | ___ | ___ | ___ | ___ |
| Assembled parts with precision | ___ | ___ | ___ | ___ | ___ | ___ | ___ | ___ |
| Prepared food | ___ | ___ | ___ | ___ | ___ | ___ | ___ | ___ |
| Drove a tractor, boat, or truck | ___ | ___ | ___ | ___ | ___ | ___ | ___ | ___ |
| **INVESTIGATIVE SKILLS** | | | | | | | | |
| Used knowledge of a science | ✓ | ___ | ___ | ___ | ___ | ___ | ___ | ___ |
| Programmed a computer | ___ | ___ | ___ | ___ | ___ | ___ | ___ | ___ |
| Researched | ✓ | ___ | ___ | ___ | ___ | ___ | ___ | ___ |
| Measured with precision | ✓ | ___ | ___ | ___ | ___ | ___ | ___ | ___ |

*Column "sample" heading (handwritten): Chosen for National Junior Honor Society*

| Investigative Skills *(continued)* | sample | 1 | 2 | 3 | 4 | 5 | 6 | 7 |
|---|---|---|---|---|---|---|---|---|
| Observed people, data, or things | ✓ | ___ | ___ | ___ | ___ | ___ | ___ | ___ |
| Used symbols, like numbers or formula | ___ | ___ | ___ | ___ | ___ | ___ | ___ | ___ |
| Used scientific or technical language | ___ | ___ | ___ | ___ | ___ | ___ | ___ | ___ |
| Used laboratory or scientific equipment | ✓ | ___ | ___ | ___ | ___ | ___ | ___ | ___ |
| Followed technical instructions | ___ | ___ | ___ | ___ | ___ | ___ | ___ | ___ |
| Tested an idea or hypothesis | ___ | ___ | ___ | ___ | ___ | ___ | ___ | ___ |
| Combined ideas in a new way | ___ | ___ | ___ | ___ | ___ | ___ | ___ | ___ |
| Read or wrote scientific reports | ___ | ___ | ___ | ___ | ___ | ___ | ___ | ___ |
| Collected and recorded scientific data | ✓ | ___ | ___ | ___ | ___ | ___ | ___ | ___ |
| Compared data | ___ | ___ | ___ | ___ | ___ | ___ | ___ | ___ |
| Analyzed something down to its parts | ___ | ___ | ___ | ___ | ___ | ___ | ___ | ___ |
| Traced problems or ideas to their source | ___ | ___ | ___ | ___ | ___ | ___ | ___ | ___ |
| Classified objects | ___ | ___ | ___ | ___ | ___ | ___ | ___ | ___ |

## ARTISTIC SKILLS

| | sample | 1 | 2 | 3 | 4 | 5 | 6 | 7 |
|---|---|---|---|---|---|---|---|---|
| Used language and grammar correctly | ✓ | ___ | ___ | ___ | ___ | ___ | ___ | ___ |
| Edited | ___ | ___ | ___ | ___ | ___ | ___ | ___ | ___ |
| Photographed | ___ | ___ | ___ | ___ | ___ | ___ | ___ | ___ |
| Used colors, spaces, and shapes | ___ | ___ | ___ | ___ | ___ | ___ | ___ | ___ |
| Painted, sculpted, or designed | ___ | ___ | ___ | ___ | ___ | ___ | ___ | ___ |
| Shaped or molded | ___ | ___ | ___ | ___ | ___ | ___ | ___ | ___ |
| Used extensive vocabulary | ___ | ___ | ___ | ___ | ___ | ___ | ___ | ___ |
| Created stories, plays, or poetry | ___ | ___ | ___ | ___ | ___ | ___ | ___ | ___ |
| Used tools like brushes, pens, chisels | ___ | ___ | ___ | ___ | ___ | ___ | ___ | ___ |
| Created artistic objects | ___ | ___ | ___ | ___ | ___ | ___ | ___ | ___ |
| Performed before an audience | ___ | ___ | ___ | ___ | ___ | ___ | ___ | ___ |
| Invented, created new ideas or images | ___ | ___ | ___ | ___ | ___ | ___ | ___ | ___ |
| Expressed thoughts and feelings | ___ | ___ | ___ | ___ | ___ | ___ | ___ | ___ |
| Taught music, acting, or dancing | ___ | ___ | ___ | ___ | ___ | ___ | ___ | ___ |
| Sang or played a musical instrument | ___ | ___ | ___ | ___ | ___ | ___ | ___ | ___ |

| Artistic Skills (continued) | sample | 1 | 2 | 3 | 4 | 5 | 6 | 7 |
|---|---|---|---|---|---|---|---|---|
| Composed or arranged music | ___ | ___ | ___ | ___ | ___ | ___ | ___ | ___ |
| Acted | ___ | ___ | ___ | ___ | ___ | ___ | ___ | ___ |

## SOCIAL SKILLS

| | | | | | | | | |
|---|---|---|---|---|---|---|---|---|
| Advised or counseled people | ___ | ___ | ___ | ___ | ___ | ___ | ___ | ___ |
| Listened intently and accurately | ✓ | ___ | ___ | ___ | ___ | ___ | ___ | ___ |
| Responded with warmth and courtesy | ___ | ___ | ___ | ___ | ___ | ___ | ___ | ___ |
| Interviewed people | ___ | ___ | ___ | ___ | ___ | ___ | ___ | ___ |
| Understood people's feelings | ___ | ___ | ___ | ___ | ___ | ___ | ___ | ___ |
| Taught or tutored | ___ | ___ | ___ | ___ | ___ | ___ | ___ | ___ |
| Worked well with team or group | ___ | ___ | ___ | ___ | ___ | ___ | ___ | ___ |
| Empowered, raised people's self-esteem | ___ | ___ | ___ | ___ | ___ | ___ | ___ | ___ |
| Served or attended | ___ | ___ | ___ | ___ | ___ | ___ | ___ | ___ |
| Helped the sick or injured | ___ | ___ | ___ | ___ | ___ | ___ | ___ | ___ |
| Helped the young, elderly, or disabled | ___ | ___ | ___ | ___ | ___ | ___ | ___ | ___ |
| Negotiated with people | ___ | ___ | ___ | ___ | ___ | ___ | ___ | ___ |
| Coached or refereed a game or sport | ___ | ___ | ___ | ___ | ___ | ___ | ___ | ___ |
| Excelled in an athletic skill | ___ | ___ | ___ | ___ | ___ | ___ | ___ | ___ |

## ENTERPRISING SKILLS

| | | | | | | | | |
|---|---|---|---|---|---|---|---|---|
| Sold products or services | ___ | ___ | ___ | ___ | ___ | ___ | ___ | ___ |
| Coordinated events | ___ | ___ | ___ | ___ | ___ | ___ | ___ | ___ |
| Raised funds | ___ | ___ | ___ | ___ | ___ | ___ | ___ | ___ |
| Ran meetings | ___ | ___ | ___ | ___ | ___ | ___ | ___ | ___ |
| Spoke to small or large groups | ___ | ___ | ___ | ___ | ___ | ___ | ___ | ___ |
| Saw a problem and acted on it | ___ | ___ | ___ | ___ | ___ | ___ | ___ | ___ |
| Computed cost of purchase | ___ | ___ | ___ | ___ | ___ | ___ | ___ | ___ |
| Talked easily with all kinds of people | ___ | ___ | ___ | ___ | ___ | ___ | ___ | ___ |
| Helped customers decide | ___ | ___ | ___ | ___ | ___ | ___ | ___ | ___ |
| Spoke or wrote clearly | ✓ | ___ | ___ | ___ | ___ | ___ | ___ | ___ |
| Made plans to achieve goal | ✓ | ___ | ___ | ___ | ___ | ___ | ___ | ___ |
| Motivated or inspired people | ___ | ___ | ___ | ___ | ___ | ___ | ___ | ___ |

| Enterprising Skills (continued) | sample | 1 | 2 | 3 | 4 | 5 | 6 | 7 |
|---|---|---|---|---|---|---|---|---|
| Made logical business decisions | ___ | ___ | ___ | ___ | ___ | ___ | ___ | ___ |
| Supervised the work of others | ___ | ___ | ___ | ___ | ___ | ___ | ___ | ___ |
| Negotiated best deals | ___ | ___ | ___ | ___ | ___ | ___ | ___ | ___ |
| Mediated between individuals or groups | ___ | ___ | ___ | ___ | ___ | ___ | ___ | ___ |
| Persuaded people or promoted an idea | ___ | ___ | ___ | ___ | ___ | ___ | ___ | ___ |
| Understood and used a large vocabulary | ___ | ___ | ___ | ___ | ___ | ___ | ___ | ___ |
| Spoke or understood a foreign language | ___ | ___ | ___ | ___ | ___ | ___ | ___ | ___ |

## CONVENTIONAL SKILLS

| | sample | 1 | 2 | 3 | 4 | 5 | 6 | 7 |
|---|---|---|---|---|---|---|---|---|
| Made decisions based on rules | ___ | ___ | ___ | ___ | ___ | ___ | ___ | ___ |
| Calculated numbers correctly | ✓ | ___ | ___ | ___ | ___ | ___ | ___ | ___ |
| Copied many numbers accurately | ___ | ___ | ___ | ___ | ___ | ___ | ___ | ___ |
| Followed record-keeping procedures | ___ | ___ | ___ | ___ | ___ | ___ | ___ | ___ |
| Operated office machines | ___ | ___ | ___ | ___ | ___ | ___ | ___ | ___ |
| Followed detailed instructions | ___ | ___ | ___ | ___ | ___ | ___ | ___ | ___ |
| Sorted papers | ___ | ___ | ___ | ___ | ___ | ___ | ___ | ___ |
| Identified errors in recorded information | ___ | ___ | ___ | ___ | ___ | ___ | ___ | ___ |
| Filed or retrieved information | ___ | ___ | ___ | ___ | ___ | ___ | ___ | ___ |
| Collected and managed money | ___ | ___ | ___ | ___ | ___ | ___ | ___ | ___ |
| Remembered detailed information | ✓ | ___ | ___ | ___ | ___ | ___ | ___ | ___ |
| Proofread | ___ | ___ | ___ | ___ | ___ | ___ | ___ | ___ |
| Dealt with people with tact and courtesy | ___ | ___ | ___ | ___ | ___ | ___ | ___ | ___ |
| Performed routine and repetitive work | ___ | ___ | ___ | ___ | ___ | ___ | ___ | ___ |

**STEP SIX:** Read over each of the skills you checked and ask yourself, "Is this a skill I enjoy using?" "Is this a skill I have used more than once?" If your answer to both questions is yes, mark the skill with a color (like red). The skills so marked are your motivated skills.

Once you have done this for all the skills you checked, lay your Skills Inventory out on a table or the floor. This will give you an "aerial view." As you look over the results, look for patterns. Which of the motivated skills are checked most often? What would you say are your motivated skills?

Nathan getting an "aerial view" of his skills.

Are most of your skills in the Realistic skills group? Artistic? You can use this information to identify occupations that might suit you. For example, if many of your skills are in the Artistic group, you can turn to that section in Chapter 5 (pp. 41-42) and find occupations that use these skills.

Did this exercise suggest a career direction to you? Or, confirm one you already have?

## A Caution

This exercise has limitations that you should think about.

- Frequently there are skills that people would enjoy using but *have not had the time or opportunity to learn*. For example, someone who lives in the city is unlikely to have the opportunity to learn the skill of driving a farm tractor. A person in a wealthy family has opportunities to learn skills that a person in a poor family does not. Someone who is older has more time to learn skills than someone who is younger. In other words, there might be skills in the Skills Inventory that you would really enjoy using once you learned them. Read over this list of skills again and circle any that you think you would like to learn.

- There are often *social pressures that discourage people from learning skills that they would really enjoy.* For example, girls are frequently discouraged from learning science and math skills, and boys are sometimes not encouraged to pursue artistic or helping/caring skills. For these reasons, it is important for you to dream, to think creatively, to explore, and to keep your options open. For more on this, see Chapter 12.

- *People often do not recognize the skills they have.* I had a college student who ran his family's hog farm for two weeks when his mom and dad were on vacation in Bermuda. He was proud of this accomplishment, but could only name one or two skills that he used! When the students and I quizzed him, we were able to identify at least a dozen skills he used. Therefore, if you can, work with someone in identifying your skills—another student or, preferably, an adult, like your teacher or parents. Describe your achievement in detail and tease those skills out! This is very important.

## THINGS YOU CAN DO

1. Try the Strength Bombardment exercise. It is fun and helpful. You do it with a group of four or five other people. The purpose is to help each other identify his or her motivated skills.

   a. Each person chooses one of his or her achievements. On a large piece of paper, the size of a poster, write the title of your achievement at the top. Below it, list what you did. For example, when I was a teen, I bought an old 1930 Ford Model A car and fixed it up. So, when I did this activity, I put at the top of my poster, "Fixed Up Model A Ford." Under this title, I listed a) repaired car body, b) sanded body and painted it, c) took off sheet metal roof and put on cloth top, and d) got engine to run. Be sure to make the letters big enough so that the people in your group can read them.

   b. Your group gets in a circle and one person volunteers to be on the "Hot Seat." That person holds up his or her poster and describes this achievement and the skills used to do it.

   c. The group's job is to identify skills the person on the Hot Seat has not mentioned. To do this, group members will need to ask for more details about the achievement. Have the Skills Inventory in front of you; it will help you discover these new skills. A recorder for the group writes down each new skill as it is discovered and, then, gives the list of skills to the person on the Hot Seat at the end.

d. Once all the skills are identified, someone else goes on the Hot Seat. Continue until everyone has been on the Hot Seat.

2. Talk with an adult, someone in your family or a friend, about their motivated skills. You will probably have to explain to them what a motivated skill is. Once they understand, I think you will be surprised at how enthusiastically they will talk about them. Ask them to describe an achievement where they used the skill.

3. It's fun to observe people discover their motivated skills. Look for people at a time when they show pleasure or pride over an achievement. Then, try to name the skill or skills they used. As a compliment to them, try saying something like, "Boy, you really know how to _____," and name the skill. See how they react. Most people enjoy this kind of compliment. This is a valuable social skill to learn.

# CHAPTER 12

## The Sky's the Limit!

**R**elax, and imagine that you are on a flight to Atlanta. As the plane rises, you hear the captain say, "Welcome to Delta Air Lines. We are pleased that you joined us. Our flight time is approximately one hour and 35 minutes, and we will arrive in Atlanta at 8:18. The weather is clear and we will have a pleasant flight. Please let the flight attendant know if there is any way we can make your trip more enjoyable. Thank you for flying Delta." Now, before you turn the page, try to imagine the pilot flying the plane. What does the person look like?

## SEX STEREOTYPES

How did you imagine the pilot? Was the pilot you visualized a man or a woman? Most people would visualize a man. Did you?

This image that we have of pilots being men is called a sex stereotype. This means that a group of people have the same mental picture of what males and females do and think. This mental picture is oversimplified and often biased. For example, nurses are usually thought of as women, not men; police officers and pilots, only as men.

Sex stereotypes can have a negative impact on you and your friends. For example, let's say you are a guy, and you like to help people and enjoy biology. Will you think of becoming a nurse? You may not even think of it. Why? Your sex stereotype about nurses keeps it out of your mind. Or, what if you do think of it, and you tell your friends or your parents? Will they laugh or question your judgment? It's possible. This ignorance, or in many cases sexism, may discourage you from going into the occupation that fits you best—one that you will really enjoy and excel in. Do you want that?

## OVERCOMING LIFE'S CHALLENGES

The purpose of this chapter is to say the following to you as strongly and as enthusiastically as I can: *Believe in yourself. You are able to reach heights you never imagined.* It's true. I know from personal experience.

When I was in school, I got "so so" grades. I was not particularly motivated. My biggest barrier was in my mind. I didn't believe in myself. I lacked self-confidence. If someone had told me I was capable of getting a doctorate degree in psychology, of becoming a university professor, I would never have believed them. Absolutely not! At that time, I didn't know if I was even capable of doing college work.

But I was lucky. One day, after I graduated from high school, I went back to see my old teachers. My English teacher, Rose Fucile, asked me what I was doing. When I told her I was working for the state as a clerk, she looked me in the eye and said firmly, "Larry, you should be in college." I can still remember that moment. I know it sounds corny, but by that statement, she forever changed my life.

Her belief in me and her telling me to "think big" made the difference. From that day on, I began to believe more in myself, and I became more ambitious. In other words, *how you think* about yourself and your future is very, very important.

There is another lesson in this story. *The people in our lives make a difference.* They influence what we believe about ourselves and our vision of the future. Just as Rose Fucile, you can encourage your friends to believe in themselves and their future. You can fight against the stereotypes that breed racism, sexism, jealousy, and ridicule.

The story also says that you want to be around people who believe in you, who have a positive outlook on life. If you find yourself with someone or a group of people who put you down, or have a negative outlook on life, make friends with someone else.

I did have one great advantage—I was an able, white male. I did not have to face the racism and prejudice that African Americans, Hispanic Americans, and other minority groups face. Sexism and sex stereotypes were not barriers to my thinking and action. I was not visually impaired or confined to a wheelchair.

Fortunately, many people who do not have my "able, white male" advantage are determined to succeed, and they do realize their dreams. They are inspirations to everyone.

Read about James Benton in Chapter 3. Did he let thoughts or stereotypes about being "blind" or a "black man" keep him back? No. He kept at it. He developed marketable skills and succeeded. Alphonso Hayes, pursued his dream of nursing even though there are few males in this profession (p. 79).

In the remainder of this chapter, you will read about others who serve as examples for all of us. I think you will be inspired. I was.

## Meet Airline Pilot Patricia Denkler-Rainey

Captain Patricia Denkler-Rainey in the cockpit one evening, after flying the plane from Denver.

Pat loves flying. She originally got the idea from watching her brother, a Marine pilot. "I got to watch him when he was flying, and I got really excited about flying." In college someone offered to teach her how to fly in a 1946 airplane. "We went up flying, and I fell in love with it. I had no radio, no instruments, just your basic airplane. You'd fly with the door open. I thought, 'This is it. This is what flying is.' I went head over heels with it. I really did."

After college, Pat went to school to get her license as an aircraft mechanic; she was the only female in the training program. "I didn't know a hammer from a screwdriver. If I was going to be doing this, I thought I should know more."

While training as a mechanic, she heard that the Navy was allowing women to enlist in their naval aviation training program. She applied, was selected, and did well in flight school. Pat was among the first of the women (seven out of about 400 men) to be trained to fly a jet fighter and land it on an aircraft carrier. She got the highest grades of all those in training.

The training of the women was kind of a secret. Superiors told Pat, "Let's not make a big deal of it. Let's just send you through, just like you're a guy, and hope nobody picks up on that it hadn't really been done before." Even the Admiral in charge of training didn't know about it.

Then it came time to land her jet on the aircraft carrier, the first woman to do this in the Navy. She was told, "Listen, this is what we've got working here. We want you to be the one to go and do this. What do you think?" Pat said, "Are you kidding? That's great!" Her landing on the ship went well, and *Pat became the first woman to carrier qualify.*

**Pat on the day she became carrier qualified.**

Carrier qualifying is one of the accomplishments Pat is most proud of. "And it wasn't because I was the first woman. That was an aside that really did not matter to me. I wanted to land on a carrier. There is nothing more challenging or more of a rush emotionally than the first time you go out there and do that. That is just a tremendous measure of ability. The whole time you're going through training, you're thinking, 'I don't know if I'll be able to do that.'"

"It was just something that I'd always wanted to do, ever since my brother had done it. And then to actually be able to realize that dream was pretty amazing. There is absolutely nothing that can take the place of doing that. And it really had nothing to do with me being a girl. . . . It was just being able, as a pilot, to do it."

After 10 years with the Navy, Pat resigned and went to fly for Delta Air Lines. "I absolutely loved being in the Navy when I went in," Pat says, but she became frustrated because she felt restricted in her attempts for advancement. It was not easy for a woman to be promoted, even if she did a good job.

Pat has flown for Delta Air Lines since 1985. After two months of training, she started as a flight engineer. About a year later she became a co-pilot, and now she flies the 204-seat Boeing 767. She is able to fly on different schedules. For example, one four-day trip might be Atlanta to Mexico City to Philadelphia to New York, and back to Atlanta; another trip might be San Diego to Seattle to Orlando. "Each trip is totally different. And you know a month ahead of time when you'll be flying. So there's no way you can get bored by the routine. That's what makes the job so fun. Plus, I really enjoy the camaraderie between the pilots, flight attendants, and passengers."

When she is not flying for Delta, she pursues a number of interests. She likes to write in her journal and play with short story ideas. She loves "little airplane flying" [like the 1946 "taildragger"she first flew]. "What I do now is work a lot with kids, teaching them to fly. And I try to work with kids that, for whatever reason, need a little boost to their egos."*

* Information and quotes from *Trailblazers Aerospace News* (Spring, 1993)

## Learning from Pat

Pat's story is inspirational. It shows you what a person can accomplish with hard work and determination. Her story also teaches us a number of other lessons. We should not let sex stereotypes prevent us from reaching our dreams—old-fashioned ideas about "men's jobs" and "women's jobs" shouldn't hold us back. And we should encourage our friends when they are thinking of going into a "nontraditional field for their sex." If a guy wants to become a nurse or a girl wants to be a firefighter, let's say, "Yes. That's great!" Everyone needs to be encouraged to work in a field they will like.

## THOMAS W. JONES

Tom Jones gives new meaning to the phrase, "You can soar to new heights."

**Tom Jones oversees the world's largest pension fund.**
**Photo courtesy of** *Black Issues in Higher Education.*

Tom is the president and chief operating officer of the largest pension fund in the world—TIAA-CREF. How large is it? More than $135 billion! Yes, he is in charge of that.

A pension fund is an organization that receives money from workers and their employers to invest for the workers' retirement. For example, each month money is deducted from my paycheck and sent to TIAA-CREF. My employer also contributes money for me each month. TIAA-CREF invests this money in stocks of companies around the world, and in things like loans to build office buildings and shopping malls. Over the years, if this money is invested wisely, it will grow in value and provide me with a lifetime retirement income. When I retire, TIAA-CREF will send me a check each month.

TIAA stands for Teachers Insurance Annuity Association, and CREF stands for College Retirement Equities Fund. More than 1.7 million people have their retirement savings invested in TIAA-CREF. They are people who work at places like colleges, universities, museums, independent schools, and libraries.

Tom has many duties as chief operating officer (COO). He helps determine TIAA-CREF's long-range strategic plans. These plans cover such things as the company's products, markets, and customer services. He oversees the development and implementation of annual plans to achieve the long-range strategic objectives. The COO also reports to the governing board on how well the company has achieved the annual plan's objectives.

Can you imagine being in charge of TIAA-CREF? To have such a great responsibility on your shoulders? Those 1.7 million people are depending on you and TIAA-CREF to invest their money wisely. What skills and personal qualities would you need? Obviously, Tom Jones is an exceptional person. He offers the following advice to young Black Americans and other minority groups with aspirations to reach the heights he has reached: "You know, it doesn't sound like much, but the real secret is, can you do the things that you know are the right things to try to do, as best as you can possibly do it, every day, day after day? Can you keep getting up to that level of excellence, that level of discipline, that level of focus, that each day you just give all you've got, and not just give it all you've got, but you're giving it for the right purposes."*

*Information and quotes are from Black Issues in Higher Education (October 24, 1994) and Black Enterprise (June, 1994).

## JoAnn Burkholder, Pioneering Scientist

In our country, we honor pioneers, people with the courage and determination to open up new frontiers. JoAnn fits that tradition in at least two ways. First, as a scientist she is opening up new areas of study in marine ecology. Dr. Burkholder, an aquatic botanist, discovered, along with her associates at North Carolina State University, a "phantom" algae responsible for mysterious kills of millions of fish. And, second, she is helping to open up science as a career for women.

It's a fact that women are concentrated in low-paying, traditionally female-dominated occupations and are often discouraged from pursuing higher paying careers in math and science occupations. JoAnn was herself frequently discouraged from entering science.

Whether you are male or female, I think you will enjoy reading about JoAnn. You can learn from her life.

### JoAnn's Remarkable Discovery

The creature JoAnn discovered has been described in numerous newspaper and magazine articles. Here are some of the ways it has been described:

Alien in our midst

Grass feeding on sheep

Tiny predator, huge prey

The cell from hell

Slumbering algae

Toxic phantom algae

Silent stalker

Phantom fish killer

Dr. Jekyll and Mr. Hyde organism

Half plant, half animal

Two scientists at North Carolina State University, Drs. Edward Noga and Stephen Smith, noticed something was killing the fish in their aquarium. Upon investigating, they found in the aquarium an unidentified, microscopic algae. They sent samples of the algae to different scientists, including JoAnn. And JoAnn and her colleagues discovered that this algae was, indeed, killing the fish.

This algae is called a dinoflagellate. Dino, in Greek, means "whirling." A dinoflagellate whirls about itself. The algae can only be seen in a microscope; at its largest, it measures about one-fifth of a millimeter. It can go at least two years without feeding. The algae can lie for years in the mud at the bottom of rivers or bays in a form called a "cyst," a minute capsule. Then, when fish are feeding above, the algae is transformed, in minutes, into dinoflagellates that swim towards the fish. The algae releases a powerful poison that kills the fish. After feeding on the dead fish, the algae changes back to cyst form and settles to the bottom of the river. During its life span, it can change into at least 15 different forms.

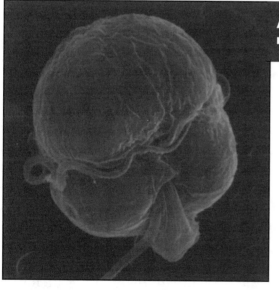

A toxic algae that has mysteriously killed millions of fish, magnified 9,000 times.

Phytoplankton are not supposed to behave like this, so many scientists questioned JoAnn's findings. However, she persisted and did more research. In the process of doing this research, she was herself temporarily poisoned. Once, after spending three hours in a laboratory working with this algae, she became disoriented, suffered stomach cramps, and had an asthma attack. For days after, she had difficulty seeing and suffered from short-term memory loss.

*Pfiesteria piscimorte*, referred to as an "ambush predator," is now accepted by scientists, thanks to JoAnn's research. It, or similar species, is thought to exist in the bottoms of rivers and bays worldwide. These species of algae are responsible for the deaths of millions of fish, and may even kill seabirds and humpback whales. Unfortunately, phosphates from fertilizers and other pollution encourage their growth.

JoAnn working in her laboratory.

### An Interview with JoAnn

LJ: What are the things that you primarily do in your job?

JoAnn: I tend to work around the clock, usually about 7 days a week. My job technically is split between teaching and research, but I have many projects going on, and I'm very active in outreach. For example, last year I was on the Governor's Coastal Futures Committee to try and understand how to better protect water quality and develop stronger policy for water quality protection on the coast. I do many different things of that sort.

LJ: What do you like most about your job?

JoAnn: I like being able to apply my research to real life problems, like how to keep the water on our coasts clean. I like that fact because it's given me the opportunity to work with the people I call "grassroots folks." These people are concerned citizens groups, high school students, middle school students, and grade school students. I explain what's happening to coastal water quality and try to get them involved in improving it.

LJ: Would "grassroots folks" also include fishers and people in the marine industry?

JoAnn: Yes. I also go to public hearings and help concerned citizens groups understand some of the issues involved, like what's wrong with pollution runoff, like urban runoff or agricultural drainage—how such pollution is going to affect the water they want to use for swimming, fishing, or boating. I try to give them help behind the scenes.

J:     As you know, girls become less involved in science in the middle and high school years even though they have the ability and interest. Do you have any thoughts or advice in this area?

oAnn:  Well, I understand. I grew up in a lower middle class, blue collar area, and I was constantly told that I should not even consider doing anything except be a secretary and a housewife, except by one person, my father.

My father never really had a son, and I loved doing the things he liked to do, but I think he would have done it anyway. I shared his interests; I went out to the field and helped him by going hunting and that kind of thing. I never really shot, but I was his "bird dog." I'd help him flush out the game. Just through those experiences he taught me to love to take a risk, to love adventure, and to love being out in the woods. I took it very seriously.

So I think it was through his influence that I ended up deciding that no matter what I heard, I could do what I wanted. I could succeed. I think that the most important thing to tell young women is to really try to understand how important it is to do what you want to do. If you really want to do something, keep at it and do not listen to negative reinforcement. Try to believe in yourself no matter what you hear. Keep telling yourself that you can do something that you really want to do. I think the most important thing that people should be trying to teach young people, young women as well as young men, is the value of taking risks and being adventurous enough to want to go out and make changes and do things. Not just to follow the traditional ways.

## SUMMARY

- Don't think in stereotypes; such thinking hurts you and your friends.

- Encourage your friends to believe in themselves and their future.

- Fight racism, sexism, and other forms of prejudice.

- Believe in yourself and your future.

- Make friends with people who are positive and who encourage you.

- Work hard; persist.

- Reach for the sky!

PART four

# LEARNING NEW SKILLS

# Reaching Your Dreams

**W**hat kind of life do you see for yourself and your loved ones? What are your dreams? Think about them for a moment. Do you dream of living in the country? in the city? at the seashore? Will you go to an office? Work outdoors? Have your own business? Travel? Own your own home? Discover a cure for cancer? Raise children? Win a great athletic event? Become a novelist?

Take out a sheet of paper and write down your dreams.

## YOU ARE CREATING YOUR FUTURE

By the decisions you make, you are creating your future. Fourteen-year-old Min Hee Choi is making decisions that will shape her future.

**Min Hee Choi has dreams for the future, and she is working hard to achieve them.**

Min Hee came to this country because her mother and father had dreams for her. A college education is hard to get in South Korea. Her family moved to the United States three years ago so she would have a better opportunity to go to college. Min Hee remembers the move: "I was scared, I couldn't speak English, and I didn't know anybody except my aunt and uncle. At elementary school, people were trying to help me because I didn't know any English. I was really thankful for that." Min Hee has worked hard to reach her goal of learning English. She used to go to the English as a Second Language classes, but now she no longer needs to.

Min Hee has a goal for the future: "I want to be a doctor when I grow up, because I want to help people with awful diseases. I want to use the money I earn to help the homeless people, and use it for my Church."

What decisions has Min Hee made? How have they shaped her future?

What you decide in the next few years will largely determine your future. Will it be a dream or a nightmare? Your future is in your own hands—in the decisions you make. You are making those decisions right now: Who shall I be friends with? Which courses should I take? How hard should I study for the exam next week? What should I do after I leave high school? Should I take drugs? Drink? Smoke? Should I date _____? Should I be sexually involved?

These are awesome decisions to make. These are scary decisions, but also exciting ones. To a large extent, you are an artist; you are creating your own life. And, you are not alone in doing this. Many people will help you: loved ones, teachers, counselors, and friends. They can give you information, new ideas, and emotional support. Ultimately, however, it is your life, and your decisions.

## POSTPONING SEXUAL INVOLVEMENT

You may be wondering, "What is this topic doing in a book on job skills?" I asked my student editors if I should include it. They were unanimous: "Yes, definitely. It's important." Sexual intercourse at this time of your life can smash your dreams.

You will make many decisions in your life. One of the most important is when you choose to begin sexual involvement. You will want to give this question serious thought.

In addition to religious beliefs, there are many other reasons for you to wait for sexual involvement.

- The risk of getting and dying from AIDS or becoming infected with a venereal disease like syphilis, gonorrhea, or herpes is real.

- Girls, you can get pregnant (half of the women between 15 and 19 who get pregnant believed the myth, "I won't get pregnant.").

- Almost 90 percent of teenage guys who get girls pregnant abandon them.

- Teens who get married most often end up divorced.

- Children of teen mothers are more likely to die and to have serious problems such as cerebral palsy, epilepsy, and mental retardation than the children of women who delay childbirth until their twenties.

- You will be a much better mother or father of your child when you are in your twenties than when you are in your teen years.

- Most teen mothers do not complete high school, earn less income as adults, are less likely to learn the job skills needed to succeed at work, and are more likely to be unemployed.

Girls hear from guys, "I'll always respect you. I really need you." What he means is he wants to use you. What he needs is the courage to be responsible. And you need another boyfriend, someone who will care and respect you enough not to put pressure on you.

What you decide to do will have a major impact on your life and on your dreams for the future. Save the joy of sexual relations until you find the right loving partner for your lifetime.

## JOB SKILLS AND YOUR DREAMS

The job you hold will have a major influence on your life. It will determine how you spend most of your time as an adult. It will affect who your friends are, whether you can buy your own home, and the kind of car you can afford. It will affect whether you can help your children financially with their education.

*Your future depends on the decisions you make about job skills.* If, for example, you decide to goof off in school and not learn needed job skills, you will likely spend your adult life working at unskilled jobs like cleaning toilets or flipping hamburgers. If, on the other hand, you decide to learn marketable job skills, you will have a bright future!

## YOU CAN REACH YOUR DREAMS

You can reach your goals by taking the following steps: Decide. Set goals. Make plans. And work to reach them.

- *Decide* that you will take control of your future. Decide what you want and go for it.

- *Set goals* and have a target to reach. Focus your energies.

- *Plan your future.* Identify the steps needed to reach your goals.

- *Work hard* to reach your goals.

Step by step. I can't see any other way of accomplishing anything.

These are the words of Michael Jordan, perhaps the most extraordinary athlete of our time. He writes as follows in *I Can't Accept Not Trying:*

> *I had always set short-term goals. As I look back, each one of those steps or successes led me to the next one. . . .When it happened, I set another goal, a reasonable, manageable goal that I could realistically achieve if I worked hard enough. . . .I knew exactly where I wanted to go, and I focused on getting there. As I reached those goals, they built on one another. I gained a little confidence every time I came through. . . .Take those small steps.*

Decide. Set goals. Make plans. Work on them. See below how these steps worked for a determined man and woman.

## A Love Story of Achievement and Fulfillment

When Herbert and Virginia Dooley were first married, they had nothing other than a love for each other and a determination to succeed. Their goal was to own a farm and raise registered beef cattle. They both had jobs, and they saved their money. Their first step was to buy four acres of land and a cow. As they saved their money, they added to the herd.

Herbert and Virginia Dooley at the state fair exhibiting one of their Charolais bulls.

Herbert picked up pop bottles to buy their first Charolais bull. "We had 10 cows and we needed a bull," Virginia remembers. "The bull was expensive. He was $1,000. Herbert would change the money he earned from the pop bottles to silver dollars. When he had 1,000 silver dollars, we bought the bull. And we went from there. It's really been a challenge."

Early in their married life, they started a janitorial service in the town of Lenoir. At the time, it was a new idea. They learned by their mistakes. They learned the skills they needed. They kept at it, and their small business grew and prospered.

LJ:     Virginia, how did you learn what you needed to raise and breed registered cattle?

Virginia: Raising cattle was our recreation and our fun; it's what we did on weekends, on holidays. We found that the cattle people are very liberal. Everywhere that we went among them, they welcomed us. They often took us out to dinner. We went to Kentucky and to Tennessee; we went all around, from farm to farm, taking the children with us. Of course, we would always make an appointment to see them.

You have to set a goal and really be devoted to it. And that's what we did. As you went along you had to learn. Sometimes you weren't told everything; you had to learn the hard way—by making mistakes. For example, they would show you the registration papers for a bull and maybe you were impressed with the blood line [the bull's ancestors]. But they might not tell you that the cows that mated with that bull had calving problems. The calves of that bull would weigh too much at birth. You see you want the cow to birth a calf weighing about 60 or 75 pounds when it's born, no more than that. The calves of some bulls weigh 100 pounds when born, which is too heavy. At that weight, both the calf and mother often die during the birth.

You have to get your feet wet, and go for it. We would read about it, talk about it, and then go to different farms to learn about it.

Herbert and Virginia were also successful in using this life project to strengthen their family. They worked together as a family. Their three daughters and son raised their own calves and exhibited them. "It's been very beneficial to our family," said Virginia. Their 26-year-old son is now continuing the tradition; he has a 60-acre farm and 25 head of cattle. I believe you will agree that the Dooleys' story is inspirational.

## TWO POWERFUL TOOLS

Two skills you want to learn are 1) goal setting and 2) planning. These two tools give you power. Learn these two skills and your future will be bright.

### Goal-Setting Skills

Goals give your life zest and purpose. They energize you. They give you a direction to focus your energies. Goals give you power.

To get the most benefit from goal setting, you need to make three kinds of goals.

- Life goals

- Intermediate goals

- Short-term goals

Let's take a look at each of these types of goals.

**Life Goals:** What kind of life do you want to have? What kind of person do you want to become? These questions are important. The answers will lead you to your life goals. We will consider two ways of answering these questions.

*First,* consider this question: "When you are 80 years old, what would you like to be able to say about yourself as you look back on your life?" Your answer will give you a clearer picture of your life goals. Take some time now and think this question over. Then, take out a piece of paper and write down your answer.

*Second,* photocopy, then, review the list of values below and rate each one from 1 to 5 as to their importance to you (5="most important," 1="unimportant"). Ask yourself, "How important is each of these to me?" Then, rate them.

| | | |
|---|---|---|
| ___ Money | ___ Friendship | ___ Helping Others |
| ___ Recognition | ___ Security | ___ Power/Authority |
| ___ Family | ___ Beauty | ___ Creativity/Self Expression |
| ___ Adventure | ___ Honesty/ Integrity | ___ Intellectual Achievement |
| ___ Travel | ___ Independence | ___ Prestige, someone admired |

Now, rank-order and list those you have rated 4 or 5, putting at the top the value that is most important to you.

These two activities should give you a clearer idea of your life goals. Use these life goals to guide you when you decide on your intermediate and short-term goals.

**Intermediate Goals:** These are the goals you have for the next three to five years, when you graduate from high school. In setting these goals, it helps to have a career direction, even though you may change it later. Once you have a career direction, you can ask, "What skills and training do I need to enter occupations in this field?" When you know, you can set more specific goals.

*Example:* Let's say your career direction is hotel and restaurant management. After some research, you find that your local community college has a two-year program in this field. You take courses like accounting, computer keyboarding, written communications, principles of marketing, and principles of food preparation. You also learn that this is a growing field (many jobs), that there are many opportunities for advancement, and that the pay is good.

Doesn't knowing these facts energize you? Give you a focus? You can see how working hard in your studies now will pay off big later. You have a clearer idea of which courses to choose. In addition, you may learn that your school has Tech Prep, which means that if you choose the right courses in high school, you can finish this program after only one year at the community college, not two!

Your intermediate goals should be to

    a. learn more about hotel and restaurant management to see if it fits you. Read more about it; talk with managers in the hospitality industry to learn the pros and cons of this occupation and how to prepare for it. Learn more about related fields.

b. learn what courses and skills are needed to prepare for this field so you can make good choices.

c. complete your training and go to work one year after graduating from high school.

d. learn the Foundation Skills (see Chapter 4).

**Short-Term Goals:** These are goals that you have for the next three to six months. You work on them daily, or at least several times a week. For example, you may want to focus on one of the Foundation Skills (see Chapters 6-9). Which of these skills do you want to work on? Perhaps your Social Skills (see Chapter 8) need work? If so, your short-term goals should be to

a. show understanding, friendliness, and empathy toward people.

b. assert yourself when appropriate.

c. take an interest in what people say and do, and why they act as they do.

You could then do a number of the activities given in this book to work on these goals. Or, you could work on one of the Special Skills related to your career direction. Below are some examples (with possible career directions in parentheses) of short-term goals for acquiring Special Skills.

a. Learn how to read the blueprints used in building houses (carpenter, plumber, electrician, architect).

b. Learn how to use a table saw safely and precisely (carpenter, cabinetmaker).

c. Learn to speak conversational Spanish (international business, translator).

d. Learn how to use a computer graphics program (graphic designer, writer).

e. Learn basics of water color painting (artist, art teacher, occupational therapist).

f. Learn First Aid (nurse, athletic trainer, emergency medical technician).

g. Learn computer keyboarding (virtually all occupations).

*Guidelines for Setting Short-Term Goals.* There are good ways and poor ways of setting goals. If you follow these guidelines, you are much more likely to succeed.

1. Your goals should be ones that you have at least a 50-50 chance of reaching. Don't set impossible goals. On the other hand, don't make them too easy. If your goals are too easy to reach, there won't be enough of a challenge. You will not feel motivated to reach them.

2. Your goals should be ones that you really want to achieve. Don't set goals that you know in your heart you really are not motivated to work for.

3. Try to make goals that are measurable. For example, for the keyboarding goal, above, a good measurable goal is to say that you will practice at least three times

a week. Goals you can count make it easy to keep track of how you are doing. This is called a *frequency count*. Another method is *time duration* where your goal is to do something for a certain length of time. For example, "I will practice keyboarding for 120 minutes each week."

4. Your goals should be ones that you can work on at least two or three times a week, preferably daily.

In summary, write down your life goals. Make intermediate and short-term goals. They will focus and energize your life.

## Planning Skills

Once you set goals you need a plan for reaching them. *How* will you accomplish your goals? Without a plan, your goals are practically worthless. For example, take the last short-term goal that I listed, "Learn computer keyboarding." How will you learn computer keyboarding? Take a course? Work from a book or a video? Get a software program to run on the computer that teaches typing skills? Have a friend tutor you?

In addition to the "how," you need to plan the "when." When will you run the software program? How many times a week? For how long each time? Setting measurable goals will help you in figuring out the "when" of your plan.

**Planning Guidelines.** Here are several important steps to follow in developing your plan:

1. Write out your goals. Be sure they follow the guidelines I listed in the previous section.

2. Record your progress. Again, using keyboarding as an example, record the number of minutes or times you practice and then add them up at the end of the week. Better yet, graph your progress.

3. Control your environment. If you wanted to lose weight, would you fill your closets and drawers with candy and potato chips? There are a number of ways you can create a positive environment. For example, work on your goal in an environment that is not distracting, that is free of loud noises or visiting friends. Or, you can create a positive social environment by joining with a friend in working on the same goal; you can support each other.

4. Reward yourself. As you progress toward your goal, figure out a way to reward yourself, for example by going to a movie or eating a treat. For the keyboarding example, the person might plan to reward him or herself after accumulating three hours of practice.

5. Plan for slipping back. There will probably be times when you do not reach your goals, or when you do not work on them as often as you planned. That's OK. Don't get discouraged. That happens to everyone. You may need to revise your goal. Perhaps it is too difficult, or not challenging enough. Perhaps you need to figure out a different approach for reaching it, or a more attractive reward.

For more on this topic, review the section on "Self-Management" in Chapter 9.

## THINKING ABOUT WORKING AFTER SCHOOL?

Whether or not to work after school is an important decision. In a book on job skills you might think I would encourage you to work after school. After all, it seems logical that working would help you. You might think that it would lead to learning valuable skills and put you into contact with adults who have a positive influence on you. It also seems logical that the money you earn could be saved for going to school after graduation.

Unfortunately, these benefits are seldom seen. Instead, a number of studies show that work after school often leads to serious, negative effects. A recent study found, for example, that the more students work after school, the more likely they are to

- Earn lower grades
- Exert less effort in school
- Spend less time on homework
- Pay less attention in class
- Use alcohol and drugs more frequently

Working students reported
- Getting into trouble at school more often
- More frequent class cutting
- More mind wandering in class
- Higher rates of delinquency

With so many students working after school, it seems "normal" that students should do this. More than 66 percent of U.S. teens are employed. Yet, it wasn't always this way. In 1960, only about 33 percent of teenagers worked. And how do we compare with other countries? In Canada, 37 percent of the students work after school; in Sweden, 20 percent; in Japan, 2 percent.

In summary, teens in the U.S. are working at low-skill jobs after school that are often bad for them, while teens in the countries we are competing with are not. And, you guessed it, the teens in these other countries are learning more than U.S. students. They are developing stronger job skills. Which decision do you think is better—to work after school or not to work?

When you consider working after school, think again. What are your alternatives? The costs? Can you decide not to work, so you will have a brighter future? If you do work, limit the number of hours you work. Don't let work and buying consume your life and your future. This is a time for fun and exploration. It's a time for learning and growing stronger.

## CREATING YOUR FUTURE

You have the power. You create your future every day by the decisions you make. Your vision, your dream for the future, will act as a compass in guiding you. The goals you set for yourself will guide you in making these decisions. Your life goals show you what to strive for. Intermediate goals give you a target to aim for, a career direction to reach. And short-term goals give you something you can work on each week. In combination, your goals and decisions give you power. You are the artist creating your life. You are on the way to reaching your dreams. The power is with you.

# Great Ways to Learn New Skills

**I**n this chapter we will look at what students like yourself are learning. I want you to see the many, many learning opportunities that await you! I want to infect you with the enthusiasm that these students have for learning! I also want you to see how it will pay off for you. That way, you can join in the fun, the value, and the challenge of learning new skills.

## GETTING STARTED

*The first step is to set goals.* You need to decide which skills you want to strengthen. Do you want to work on the Foundation Skills—one of the social , responsibility, visualization, or listening skills? Or, perhaps you want to learn one of the Special Skills.

*The next step is to plan how you will learn these skills.* Will you sign up for a course? Go to an evening course in your community? Join a club? Have a friend teach you? Work on one of the learning activities in this book? Combine reading and watching videos with practice? Interview a person who has the kind of job that you think you want?

In this chapter we will look at four areas of opportunity.

- Volunteer Work

- School Activities

- Clubs

- School-to-Work Transition Programs

## VOLUNTEER WORK

Volunteer work is a rewarding opportunity to develop the habit of helping others. You can learn such valuable job skills as social, leadership, teamwork, and cultural diversity skills.

### In the Community

Here are some of the volunteer activities that teens have done in our city: plant flowers and trees to beautify the city, run errands for the elderly, do play activities with children in daycare centers, participate in clean-ups of the environment, help out with the Special Olympics, and read to and write for the elderly in nursing homes. To learn more about volunteering, call your city community services department or the voluntary action center for United Way.

### In Your School

I am sure that a number of clubs in your school do community service work. Key Club is a well known community service group; their motto is "Caring—Our Way of Life." At Leesville Road High School, the Key Club sponsors a tutor/mentor program designed to help elementary school students succeed. It's a great opportunity to learn teaching skills.

**Betsey Roberts gives Tiffany McLamb a tip on how to improve her reading.**

Betsey meets with Tiffany McLamb each week to give her encouragement and tips on how to improve her reading.

LJ:      How do you feel about what you're doing with her?

Betsey:  I'm really enjoying it. Ever since elementary school, I've been a peer tutor in some way, and I just enjoy working with her.

         Right now I'm thinking of doing something along the lines of teaching, and I'm more or less using her as a guide to whether I would be successful doing that, or whether I wouldn't enjoy it. But, so far, so good.

LJ:      Is this program something that you would recommend to other students?

Betsey:  Oh, yeah. It gives you a good experience. I think it gives you good insight. I wish we had programs in our schools where we could really go on-site and look at what different jobs are; I think through this tutoring program I can get a feel for what the education field might be like.

## SCHOOL ACTIVITIES

School offers many opportunities to learn valuable skills. Here are two examples.

### Peer Mediation

Students in many schools are learning valuable mediation skills. These skills are used to help students (their peers) who are in conflict with each other overcome their differences. As the dictionary says, mediation is an "intervention between conflicting parties to promote reconciliation, settlement, or compromise."

In the photo below, Nick Grannan and LaChaun Anderson talk about their experience as peer mediators with school counselor Olivia Day. Nick and LaChaun have really enjoyed being mediators. Olivia has trained many students in peer mediation and is a strong believer in its value.

**Nick Grannan and LaChaun Anderson share with Olivia Day their experiences as peer mediators.**

## Sports

Sports builds skills in teamwork and self-discipline. These are some of the benefits that the members of Coach Robert Schmalfeld's football team felt they had gained from being on the team. Coach Schmalfeld is good at working with his players, and they appreciate that.

Coach Robert Schmalfeld talks with some of his players about the next game.

Many adults I know speak fondly of their involvement with a sport when they were in school, and the benefits they received. Is that an opportunity you want to explore?

## CLUBS

Do you want to have fun? Make friends? Strengthen your skills? Clubs are a great way to go. And there are many clubs to choose from. I counted 40 clubs and organizations in the student handbook for one Raleigh high school. And, of course, this number does not include all the clubs *outside* of school!

In this section, I will give you an idea of some of the possibilities. You will learn what other teens are doing. I think you will find it inspiring. I did!

## 4-H

The mission of 4-H is "To help youth grow and develop through learn-by-doing experiences." There are many projects, programs, and events you can be a part of; here is a sampling.

| | | |
|---|---|---|
| Peers Empowering Peers | Camping | Small Animals |
| Horses and Ponies | Electricity | Learn to Earn |
| Career Exploration | Sheep | Cultural Heritage |
| Child Care | Photography | CareerSmarts |

Below are some personal stories of 4-H members.

**Lisa Young** signed up for TRYACT, a 4-H performing arts troupe that created and performed a puppet show to teach skin cancer prevention to elementary school chil-

dren. "Although we reached our goal of performing for 100 people, I'll be satisfied if I make a difference to just one child. If kids stay out of the sun between 11 and 2, wear sunscreen, and don't get skin cancer because of our 4-H efforts, then I will have achieved something really worthwhile." Lisa Young, age 17, Lucky Lions 4-H Club, Raleigh, NC

**Kim VanLoton** who attended the Southern Region 4-H Textile and Furniture Symposium, wants to be an interior decorator. 4-H offers Kim the chance to prepare for the demands of a career before she goes to college. "Sometimes 4-H projects and conferences get really hard. After I have finished them, I look back on what I have accomplished and I'm really glad I didn't give up. I've won a state prize and my leaders have helped me reach my goals. No matter how much you achieve in 4-H, there's always a higher standard to reach for—always. After all, the 4-H motto is 'To Make the Best Better.'" Kim VanLoton, age 16, Harrellsville, NC

**Jennifer TenEyck** lives with her family on the Erwindale Farm in Wildwood, New York. She is 14 and a ninth grader. I met her at the state fair. We were in a big building filled with the smell of cattle, hay, and manure, and the sounds of cattle mooing and an occasional rooster crowing. People were everywhere, excited and happy—ranchers moving their cattle to the show ring and fairgoers pointing and talking about the big bulls and cows they were seeing. After meeting Jennifer's mom (she gave me a big homemade chocolate chip cookie) and dad, we started talking about Jennifer's cattle and 4-H.

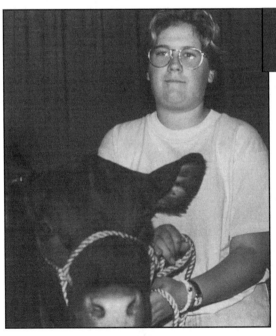

**Jennifer TenEyck proudly shows off one of the red angus bulls she raised.**

LJ:      What kind of cattle do you raise, Jennifer? And, what do you like about raising cattle?

Jennifer: They are red angus cattle. I enjoy raising them. They're easy to take care of; they're really simple and most of the time they're really calm.

LJ:      Do you enjoy being in 4-H?

Jennifer: Yes, it's fun! My mom's the leader, so I'm going to join two clubs this year, and I was in two clubs last year.

LJ: What do you like about being in a 4-H?

Jennifer: Getting to work with other people. We work on livestock judging and with the cattle, pigs, and lambs, and doing craft projects.

LJ: Do you think that being in a 4-H club will help you later in life?

Jennifer: Oh, yes. It helps you know how to get your goals together and you learn how to work with other people. We went to a retirement home last year and we planted trees with the older people. It was fun.

## North Carolina Governor James B. Hunt

The governor of North Carolina is an outstanding example of someone who made the most of his opportunities while in school.

Governor James B. Hunt of North Carolina, whose self-confidence and skills were greatly strengthened by the kinds of activities we are discussing.

"My involvement in extracurricular activities [those activities done outside of the classroom] has been a tremendous asset to me during my years as a farmer, a lawyer and as a Governor. Not only did these experiences give me the chance to meet new people—including my wife, Carolyn, who I met at a National Grange Youth Conference—but they also gave me a chance for new experiences and new opportunities.

"My activities in high school included the Future Farmers of America (FFA) and the North Carolina Grange youth program. Taking part in both these organizations gave me a better understanding of the issues facing North Carolina's farmers and the important role that agriculture and agribusiness play in our state's economy. They also helped prepare me for public service.

"Also during high school, I was fortunate to be a member of an FFA parliamentary procedure team. My family likes to tell the story about me giving campaign-style stump speeches as a youngster on the back of a tractor on the farm.

James B. Hunt, Jr., weighing milk from the FFA dairy cow.

"Some of my other high school activities included serving as senior class president, class valedictorian and quarterback of the football team. I was also captain of the basketball team, yearbook editor and a member of Boys State and Boys Nation (Washington, D.C.).

"Those activities helped build a strong foundation for my years as a student at North Carolina State University, where I was awarded the Outstanding Senior Award, and served two years as student body president and vice-president.

"All those experiences helped build my self-confidence, and helped prepare me for the challenges I would face later on—as a husband and father, as a lawyer, farmer and politician. Working with others, learning to see things from their viewpoint, setting goals and working to meet them and facing new challenges—these are all things I learned from those experiences."

## Raleigh Youth Council: Parks and Recreation Department

I thought parks and recreation departments were only involved in sports—basketball, soccer, and swimming. Was I ever surprised to learn that they are much more. They have programs that will empower you and exciting opportunities for strengthening your abilities and your self-confidence.

I asked some young people in the Raleigh Youth Council (RYC), "What does RYC mean to you?" They made comments like, "It's too much for words!" and "It's a way to have a lot of fun and help others."

Why are these teens so enthusiastic about the RYC? I began to understand the reason when I went to a weekend retreat they were having. It was out in the woods in an old Boy Scout lodge. The fire was burning in the fireplace, and the members were gathered together on the floor, in a semicircle. They were "brainstorming," an important problem-solving skill. They were to think freely of any activities that RYC might do, as rapidly as they could. No "put downs" allowed. Their youth advisor was writing down their ideas on large sheets of paper on an easel. In the next photo, you can see these large sheets of paper attached to the wall.

**Dwayne Patterson, left, the RYC advisor, is discussing activity ideas with Dawn Michael and Zack Mazer.**

Here are just a few of the ideas they listed, just as they wrote them. I'm not sure what some of them meant, but maybe you can figure them out.

| LEADERSHIP | EDUCATION | SERVICE |
| --- | --- | --- |
| Ropes course | Diversity Nite | Habitat for Humanity |
| Youth leadership workshops | Road trip | PEPI—Pullen Park |
| Personality type tests | Self-Defense | Homeless Shelters |
| "Get to know me" nite | Car class (auto mechanic) | Elder/Shut-in care |
| Public speaking workshops | Tai-Chi | Boys & Girls Clubs |

RYC has an outstanding advisor, Dwayne Patterson. He describes RYC as "a place where students can come and have wholesome, exciting, and serious fun while maturing into adulthood."

Here are few RYC projects.

*Youth-in-Business Day.* In this project, students get to "job shadow" an adult at their work for a day. This is an exciting and valuable way to learn about work. In Chapter

10, I describe how Kai Cheng did this with Sandra White, an engineering technician at Carolina Power and Light.

*Project Graduation.* This project organized a highly successful all-night alcohol and drug-free graduation celebration for seniors graduating from high school.

*Teen Helpcard.* Members have a small card printed each year that gives the telephone numbers of free or low cost services for teens in the county. Phone numbers are printed under headings like Alcohol and Drug Abuse, Child Abuse and Neglect, Health Services, and Youth Groups. More than a thousand of these cards are printed each year. They are passed out to students in schools, doctors' offices, and libraries.

The ideas for these projects, like all RYC projects, come from the student members.

Obviously, many other clubs have fine programs. There just is not enough space in this book to describe them all. I hope these brief descriptions of clubs will encourage you to explore and see what is out there. There are many opportunities to learn valuable job skills.

## SCHOOL-TO-WORK TRANSITION PROGRAMS

Do you want to take courses where you learn valuable job skills? Skills that prepare you for good jobs? Programs that prepare you for jobs in electronic servicing, surveying, or medical laboratory technology? Or, jobs in medical assisting or business administration? In this section, we will look at the following exciting programs:

- Youth Apprenticeships

- Vocational and Technical Education

- Tech Prep

- Cooperative Education

### Youth Apprenticeships

Do you want to learn valuable job skills while going to high school and be hired during the summer to use these skills? Do you want to receive a high school diploma and a certificate of competency that is highly valued by employers? Then, you will want to find out if there are any youth apprenticeships in your community.

Let's take a look at one of these programs. I know you will be impressed. In 1993, Siemens Energy & Automation, Inc. joined with the Raleigh school system to create an apprenticeship training program to prepare high school students for the electrical/electronics field. Students are in the program during their junior and senior years at East Wake High School. For these two years, 12 students meet for two hours each day to hear a classroom lecture and then work in a hands-on instruction lab where they apply what they learn. In this lab, they work in four work clusters to encourage teamwork and to receive specialized training. During the summer break, they work for pay at the Siemens plant (which manufactures electrical and electronic equipment like circuit breakers and motor controls). At the end of the program, the students receive a Siemens Apprenticeship Training Skills certificate in electrical/electronics technology. Students may then apply for full-time employment with Siemens or other companies in the electrical industry, apply the tech prep credits they earn toward an associates degree at our local community college, or apply to more advanced training programs in college.

"We wanted students who are willing to seriously commit to this program because we want it to work for them," says Barry Blystone, director of training for Siemens. "In exchange, the students will be developing career skills that are of great value to employers."

Siemens' youth apprenticeship program is teaching students valuable job skills.

I asked Nicole Smith, one of the Siemens students, how she got interested in this program.

Nicole:  I got interested because my future plans are to become an engineer, and the program really sounded as if it would help me develop my career.

LJ:  Can you tell me what the program is like?

Nicole:  The class itself is two class periods, and the first class period we may talk and discuss the lab before we actually do it. The teacher will fill us in about the product that we're to produce, and then we'll go to the lab and do different experiments, like working with metal. Right now we're working with metals and getting familiar with the drill press and saw and different metal working equipment.

LJ:  How would that be used in a person's work, do you think?

Nicole:  I think the sawing and filing teaches us patience and good working skills. You really have to be precise with your work and put forth a lot of quality.

LJ:  Would you recommend this program to other students?

Nicole:  Yes. I think that it opens doors to different opportunities later on in life.

Jess Petrosky and Nicole Smith work together in analyzing an electrical circuit.

LJ:    Jess, how did you get interested in the program?

Jess:  My electronics teacher recommended me for it.  She said I would be good for the program.

LJ:    Have you always had an interest in electronics?

Jess:  I like working with my hands.  I don't like the classroom, going in there and reading books.  I like doing stuff with my hands and working.

LJ:    Do you work with your hands a lot in this course?

Jess:  Yes, definitely.

LJ:    Is this program going to help you in the future?

Jess:  Yes.  If I ever need to do electrical work in my house or if for some odd reason I don't make it in college, I'll definitely have a job with Siemens.

If a youth apprenticeship program appeals to you, talk with your school counselor to find out what is available.  Be sure to ask how you can prepare so you will have a good chance of being selected for the program and succeeding in it.  Choosing the right courses and doing your best in them is important.

## Vocational and Technical Education

These programs prepare you for employment when you graduate from high school.  They can also give you a strong foundation for continuing your education at your community college.  They have a strong emphasis on learning valuable job skills, including the Foundation Skills that we have discussed in this book.

There is not enough space to describe them in detail, but I have listed the seven program areas in North Carolina.  Your state will have similar offerings.

1. Agricultural Education

2. Business Education

3. Marketing Education

4. Health Occupations Education

5. Home Economics Education

6. Technology Education

7. Trade and Industrial Education

These programs offer many great opportunities to learn valuable job skills. To encourage you to learn more about them, I would like to give you an example of what you can learn.

Jennifer McKagan is learning valuable computer skills.

Jennifer McKagan is in a business computer applications course and is learning how to write computer programs of her own. This course is part of the Business Education program. The display you see on her computer screen is part of a computer program she designed to help students when they use one of the computerized graphic programs. Students use these graphic programs to make presentations, like a written report. For example, her program will teach users how to use color effectively. With the tremendous use of computers in our daily world, can anyone doubt that Jennifer is learning valuable job skills? This is one example of the great opportunities for learning valuable skills in vocational and technical education programs. Check them out!

## Tech Prep

In this exciting option, you prepare yourself for a highly skilled technical job in areas like automation/robotics, computer operations, business administration, or nursing. Tech Prep is a program that combines the courses you take in high school with those you take at a community or technical college. All students learn valuable skills in math, science, communication, and technology.

In our school system, for example, there are three areas in which you can study: engineering/technology, business/marketing, and health/human services. Students studying in the health/human services area, for example, begin taking courses in the 10th grade, like algebra, biology, and introduction to health occupations. They finish the program at the end of two years in community college with an associate degree in an area like radiologic technology or registered nursing.

When you graduate from high school, you have the option of going to a four-year college or university if you have chosen your courses carefully and done well in them. It is very important that you talk with your school counselor, parents, and teachers as you go through high school so that you can develop a career direction and take the right courses.

## Cooperative Education

In this program, you actually work during the school day and receive wages and school credit. You normally have to be in the 11th or 12th grades. In your place of work, you learn valuable job skills from a skilled craftsperson who supervises your work. You are able to use what you learn in school in an actual job. Doesn't that sound great? There are a number of job areas where you might work and learn. For example, carpentry, automotive technology, drafting, and cosmetology. Talk with your teachers or school counselor to learn more.

## SUMMARY

There are many great ways you can build your skills. Many excellent learning activities are described in Chapters 6 through 9. In this chapter, we looked at the exciting ways that students are learning skills through volunteer work, clubs, courses, and vocational programs.

Of course, there are many other possibilities. For example, hobbies, like amateur radio. I'm a "ham" (call sign KD4IRV), and I see teens having great fun in this hobby, and learning valuable skills.

So, get involved. Look for ways to strengthen your Foundation Skills. Use your "motivated skills" (Chapter 11) to identify learning opportunities that appeal to you. Join in the fun. Become stronger. Learn new skills!

# Learning Skills after High School

**A**s you set goals and plan ahead, it is important to know what your options are for learning skills after high school. There are six basic options: on-the-job training, apprenticeship, private business or trade school, four-year college, military, or community college. I will describe the first five briefly, and then go into detail describing the opportunities you have at your community college.

### ON-THE-JOB TRAINING

Nearly all companies will provide you with some training. It may be short—a few days—or much longer. When you consider a job, the amount of training you will receive is an important consideration. You want to work for someone who will help you build your skills. Be sure to ask about what training opportunities they offer. Aim for getting a job that helps you learn *marketable skills*.

### APPRENTICESHIP

An apprenticeship is a three- to four-year program that allows you to learn an occupation from an experienced worker. Some occupations that offer apprenticeships include bricklayer, cabinetmaker, camera repairer, machinist, meat cutter, and plumber. Many of these programs are run by unions. You will need to ask what entry requirements they have. For a list of apprenticeable occupations, see the *Guide for Occupational Exploration* or the *Complete Guide for Occupational Exploration*. Call your state department of labor for information about programs in your state.

## PRIVATE BUSINESS OR TRADE SCHOOL

Some private schools offer short-term training in such occupations as truck driving, paralegal, cosmetology, radiologic technology, massage, and nursing. When considering these schools, check on costs, length of training, and how successful graduates have been in getting jobs.

## FOUR-YEAR COLLEGE

Your school counselor and school librarian will have information on colleges and universities. You can compare the different colleges by looking at such things as location, cost, financial aid, majors offered, and admission requirements.

## MILITARY

Work for Uncle Sam and get training, pay, room and board, and benefits. Talk with your parents and develop a list of questions before you meet with a military recruiter. Here are some suggestions.

1. What is the length of time I would stay in service?

2. What specific jobs do you have available at this time? What type of training will I get for these jobs? How can I be assured I will get the job I request?

3. How do you determine if I am qualified for a specific job?

4. What civilian jobs will my military training be useful for?

5. What benefits (education and others) are available to me after I finish my service term?

6. If I really can't adjust, is it possible to leave?*

*Adapted from NCSOICC's "Career Choices in North Carolina."

## LEARNING SKILLS AT YOUR COMMUNITY COLLEGE

A community college is an excellent place to build on your skills. I will describe the community college in some detail because I want to be sure you do not overlook its opportunities.

You have a number of options at a community college. For example, you can complete the first two years of your four-year college degree there. You can also get valuable job training that leads to good jobs.

I can speak from personal experience. The first "college" I went to was American River Junior College in California. Quite frankly, I didn't know if I could succeed in college work. At ARJC I learned valuable skills, like how to write well. In addition to skill-building, I gained the self-confidence I needed to go on for further education. In addition, the cost was low; I could afford to go to school. ARJC changed my life. It gave me a brighter future.

In North Carolina, programs are offered in the 11 job training areas listed below. Some of the programs in each training area are also listed. Your state will have similar programs.

## Job Training Programs

**Agricultural and Natural Resources.** These programs will prepare you for jobs in feed and fertilizer plants and nurseries. They will prepare you for work in poultry hatcheries, forest services and industries, water and waste water treatment plants, and animal care and recreation firms.

**Art and Design.** These programs train you for such jobs as designer, interior decorator, advertising artist, photographer, illustrator, and draftsperson.

**Business.** Do you think you would like to work in accounting, management, sales, banking, real estate, finance, insurance, manufacturing, transportation, or computer operations? If you do, then take a look at the programs in this area.

**Construction.** These programs prepare you for such construction jobs as carpentry, plumbing, and air conditioning and heating installation and repair. Or, you may become a technician in such areas as environmental engineering, architecture, or civil engineering.

**Educational.** These programs are for you if you are interested in teaching, working, and communicating with people.

**Electrical/Electronics.** These programs lead to career opportunities in communication electronics (radio, television, and radar) and industrial and medical electronics.

**Health.** Want to work in a dentist's or doctor's office, medical clinic, or hospital? These programs will give you the skills you need.

**Mechanical-Manufacturing.** These programs will prepare you for doing mechanical work in manufacturing. In these jobs, individuals repair, maintain, and make tools and machines.

**Public Service.** These programs prepare you for jobs that require you to protect the public, rehabilitate juvenile delinquents, or provide information.

**Service.** Training in this area leads to jobs in recreation, funeral service, cosmetology, foodservice, hotel and restaurant management, and legal services.

**Transportation.** These training programs prepare you for maintaining, repairing, and operating motorized equipment, including automobiles, trucks, airplanes, and ships.

As you can see, community colleges offer you a lot! Three important points to keep in mind when considering community college are the following:

1. The skills you learn today—in subjects like math, science, and English—are needed in these community college programs. Do well now and you will be prepared for the future.

2. It is not too early to learn about community college programs. Call your local community college to learn what programs they offer. They will be pleased you called, and they will send you free materials describing their programs.

3. Ask to see if your high school has a Tech Prep program. If it does, find out the details. You may be able to begin preparing in high school for the community college programs I listed above.

## Personal Stories

I spent an afternoon at Wake Technical Community College talking with students in several programs. I think you will find their stories interesting and helpful.

John F. Degele is in the Tool and Die Making program. In this program, John will learn such things as how to read blueprints, set up and operate all machine tools, cut and grind to within .0002 per inch, and operate computer numerical control (called CNC) machines (these machines are also discussed in Chapter 3).

**John Degele listens to his teacher Jerry Boone explain how to operate this CNC vertical milling machine.**

LJ:     What do you like about this work?

John:   I like the hands-on work. I like taking a chunk of steel indoors and making a tool out of it that will make millions of parts that are within thousands of an inch of one another. That's satisfying.

LJ:     John, are the skills you are learning marketable?

John:   Oh, yes. There is a strong demand for tool-and-die makers. Starting out, many are paid more than beginning engineers. Many start their own shops.

Jerry:  I have calls from employers all the time wanting to hire our graduates. They can get a good job, indoors, regular work, and they are paid very well. A lot of the people in the field now are aging out. They are retiring or going into management. This is a great field for young workers. There's something special about being able to take the knowledge between your two ears and get it to your fingertips to produce a product you can actually see.

An example of a tool that John might create is an injection mold. Two pieces of steel are precisely cut to fit together and form a cavity inside. Hot molten plastic is injected inside and allowed to cool. Some examples of products produced with an injection mold are the seats of plastic chairs and plastic toys.

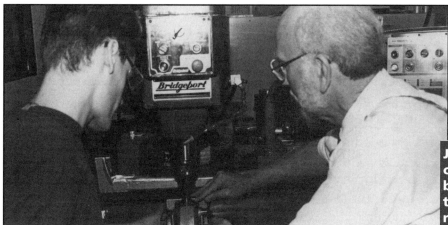

Jerry shows John the precise way to place the metal block that will be cut by this vertical milling machine.

Kerwin Yost will receive an Associate in Applied Science degree in automation/robotics technology. With his training in this field, he will be able to operate, maintain, and repair automated equipment and robots that are used in many factories across our country and, according to Kerwin, "You can do sales of any of these components, if you wanted to get in the sales trade."

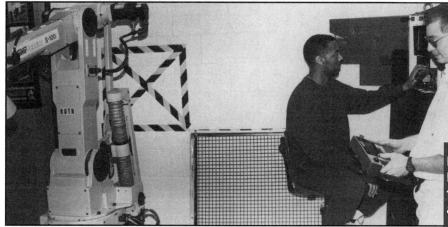

Kerwin Yost, left, and Keith Bridgman program the computer that operates the robot.

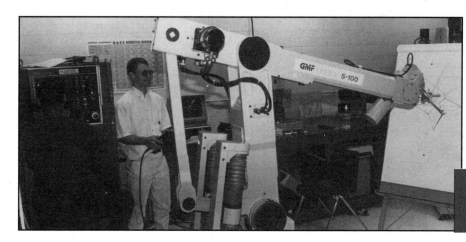

Kerwin and Keith command the robot to draw a star.

LJ:     Kerwin, what about this field appeals to you?

Kerwin: It's the future, this is the future. Backbreaking jobs are going by the wayside. Robots don't get sick, they don't need time off, they don't have children, and they don't need health insurance. They work 7 days a week, 24 hours a day. It's the wave of the future. If you don't keep up, you are going to fall behind. The earning potential is good. You can make a lot of money. It's possible. And the employment outlook is good.

Kerwin agreed that workers need marketable skills, a lesson that he learned the hard way. In an earlier job, Kerwin learned skills that were unique to the military. They were not transferable to other jobs. Employers could not use these skills. He couldn't market them. He couldn't get hired to use them.

Andra Elizabeth Taylor has enjoyed being in the Air Conditioning, Heating, and Refrigeration program. In this program, she is learning how to install and repair these systems. She also is learning how to "size" a system. This means that she is learning how to determine how powerful a furnace or air conditioner is needed for a building when you consider how much space there is, how many windows there are, and other factors. Problem solving is an essential skill in this work.

Andra Taylor is testing this furnace unit to find out why it is not working.

According to the instructor, Michael Kite, there are many more job openings in this field than there are people to fill them. And technicians in this field are well paid.

## SUMMING UP

Whether you are in middle school or high school, now is the time to be preparing for when you graduate from high school. Set goals and plan ahead. Know your options. In this chapter we have looked at six options: on-the-job training, apprenticeship, private business or trade school, four-year college, military, and community college.

Plan ahead. Take the courses now that will allow you to choose later. Many students get caught because they take the easiest classes. They can't get into the program they want because they have not taken the required courses.

The same thing can happen when you don't do your best now. If you goof off now, you will be closing doors to your future.

If you think about it, this is a great time to be alive. Look at all the possibilities you have! There are many, many ways of learning skills that you will enjoy, that will make you strong and successful.

PART five

# THESE ARE MY SKILLS

# CHAPTER 16

## Job Skills Portfolio

**I**magine a portfolio of your skills. Imagine a large, attractive envelope or holder where you store proof of your achievements! Certificates of achievement. Photos. Records of things you have done, of things that you feel good about. Your plans for the future. What could be more personal? Uplifting? And give you a greater sense of direction?

You have a lot to be proud of, even to brag about. You have accomplished many things over these years. You have developed many skills. You have done many good things.

Why not create your own portfolio? Like an artist, architect, or graphics designer?

### MEET MEREDITH BAGERSKI

Meredith is a student in graphics at North Carolina State University School of Design. I asked her if I could interview her and take a photo of her portfolio for the book. "Of course!" she replied enthusiastically. "Especially since it is for middle and high school students."

**Meredith Bagerski showing her portfolio with the art work she keeps in it.**

LJ:        Meredith, please tell me about your portfolio. Why do you have one? What kinds of things do you keep in it? What do you use it for?

Meredith: I have it to carry my designs and drawings, to keep them safe and clean so they won't rub against other things that might get them dirty. Basically to keep them safe. The things I put in the portfolio are the things I'm going to use to show either an interviewer or a prospective client, and I pick the ones that show the diversity of all my work. They show different things from different levels of skill, from easy simple things to the most difficult things.

LJ:        And you could use this, say, if you were looking for a job?

Meredith: A job or school, or contest, competitions. I use it for that. It's just to carry my stuff in; it's real handy.

LJ:        You mentioned using it maybe for a client, if you were to do something for someone?

Meredith: Yes, to bring it out and have my designs and drawings in nice, clean order.

## HOW CAN A JOB PORTFOLIO HELP ME?

Like Meredith, you can use your portfolio for

- *Safekeeping.* Keep in it the achievements about which you are most proud. This way you keep them together; you won't forget or lose them.

- *Planning.* You can review what you have accomplished over the past few months and years and plan ahead. You can see how you are progressing toward the goals you have set for yourself. Has your career direction changed? Stayed the same? It's a good idea to review your portfolio each month.

- *Pleasure.* Yes. It's satisfying to see what you know, what you have achieved.

- *Show to Others.* If you apply for a position, you can use your portfolio to show that you have the skills needed. For example, say you wanted to mow your neighbors' lawns to earn extra money. Imagine how impressed they would be if you showed them photos of your work and letters of recommendation from other neighbors praising your work!

You can also show your portfolio to family and friends. A great idea is to review your portfolio with your parents/guardians every two or three months. Or, how about showing it to family members you visit during holidays?

## PREPARATION FOR THE ADULT WORLD

Developing a portfolio is an important step toward becoming an adult and entering the world of work. Let's go back to Meredith. She won't be hired as a graphics designer unless she has the skills an employer wants. If she is self-employed, she can't sell her services unless the buyer believes she has the skills needed. This is true of all workers. If you can't show employers you have the skills they need, they won't hire you. By developing a portfolio, you are getting practice in presenting skills to others, an important skill to learn.

## DEVELOPING A JOB SKILLS PORTFOLIO

There are many ways you can construct a job skills portfolio. Start off simple. Then, as you build on it, you can expand it.

Begin by creating two categories: "Career Planning" and "Skills." You will put the materials in your portfolio in one or the other category. One way to do this is to use two 8½ by 11 inch folders, one labeled Career Planning, and the other Skills. Or you may want to take a three-ring binder and divide it into these two categories. However you choose to do it, make it look sharp! Make it something you will really feel proud of.

Let's take a look at what goes in each of the two categories.

### Career Planning

In this category you keep a record of your career planning efforts: the goals you have and the information you have collected about your career direction. These goals are listed below.

**Life Goals:** This would include what you write about your values when you read Chapter 13, the most important roles you see yourself playing, and what you would like to say about yourself at age 80.

**Intermediate Goals:** Place here what you write on this topic in Chapter 13: your projected career direction, the occupations you want to learn more about, the academic program you will follow in high school, and what your educational plans are after high school.

**Career Assessments:** The results of any aptitude or achievement tests or career interest inventories you took go here. Be sure to include the results from Chapter 5, when you assess your resemblance to the six personality types: Realistic, Investigative, Artistic, Social, Enterprising, and Conventional.

**High School Program:** Which program will you pursue? College Prep? Tech Prep? I have created a form on which you can record this information. Fill it out at the beginning of each school year, and any time your plans change. You will find this form at the end of the chapter. Make a photocopy for your use.

**Plans after High School:** At the beginning of each school year, decide what your plans are and write them down on the form at the end of the chapter. Update the form as needed. In addition, keep a list of the occupations and occupational fields that are attractive to you.

**Career Exploration:** Record your efforts at learning about occupations. This could include your notes from interviewing someone in your field of interest, volunteer work in your area of career interest, career reference books you consulted, videos you viewed, or information you got on high school academic programs like Tech Prep. Use the form at the end of this chapter.

**Occupational Profiles:** These profiles are discussed in Chapter 10 (see p. 131). Place them in this section.

## Skills

In this category, keep information on the skills you have and the ones you want to learn.

**Motivated Skills:** The results of what you do in Chapter 11 go here: a list of your achievements, your top seven achievements, their description, the results of your Skills Inventory, and the occupations that these skills suggested.

**Foundation and Special Knowledge Skills:**

1. *Skills Assessment:* Place here the self-assessments at the ends of chapters 6, 7, 8, and 9. Put your ratings from these assessments in this section.

2. *Skill Learning Activities:* The notes or other results of the activities you did to strengthen the different Foundation Skills go here. See the form at the end of this chapter. If you wanted, you could break this category down further: Basic Skills, Thinking Skills, People Skills, and Personal Qualities.

3. *Proof of Skills:* Include here any information that shows you have skills. For example, if you did volunteer work at a hospital, you could include a brochure describing the hospital, your job description, photos of you working, evaluations of your work, or recommendations from your supervisor. You could include course grades, certificates earned (like Red Cross Life Saving), awards, offices held, committees chaired, programs you participated in (e.g., conflict resolution, peer mediation, tutoring), part-time/summer work experience, attendance records, performances given, and so on.

One of the students who created a portfolio, LaChaun Anderson (p. 168), included the clothing designs she created. That's a good example of an item to put in this section.

Jackson Helms shows off his job skills portfolio: "I thought it was fun to make.  And I think it can really be helpful."

I know you will find creating a job skills portfolio satisfying.  It will help you as you chart a career direction and learn the skills to succeed in the future.  Good luck and have fun!

THESE ARE MY SKILLS

## ACADEMIC PROGRAM IN HIGH SCHOOL

**NAME**_____     **DATE**_____

Check the one that applies:

_____ College Prep (Take the courses needed to enter a 4-year college)

_____ Tech Prep (Take courses in both high school and community college. You finish the program one to two years after high school with a degree or certificate from the community college.):

       _____ Business Management

       _____ Engineering Technology

       _____ Environmental/Life Sciences

       _____ Human/Social Services

       _____ Industrial Technology

       _____ Marketing Management

       _____ Medical/Health Professions

       _____ _____

_____ Vocational Training in _____

(This is a program that prepares you for a job when you graduate from high school. Examples of these programs are: carpentry, masonry, air conditioning & refrigeration, electronics, welding, auto mechanics, auto body repair, technical drafting, and cosmetology.)

_____ Other _____

## PLANS AFTER GRADUATION

**NAME**_____   **DATE**_____

Check the one that applies:

_____    Work

_____    Part-time

_____    Full-time

_____    Begin apprenticeship or job-training program (In these programs you learn an occupation under the supervision of an experienced worker; for example: auto-body repairer, bookbinder, firefighter, locksmith, or refrigeration mechanic.)

_____    Military, Branch: _____

_____    1-year Community College Program

_____    2-year Community College Program

_____    Technical or Vocational School

_____    4-year College

Possible occupations that I am considering at this time:

_____    _____

_____    _____

_____    _____

_____    _____

_____    _____

_____    _____

_____    _____

## CAREER EXPLORATION

People who seek out career information—learning about themselves and their career options—are much happier with their jobs.

Actions (write in the name & date for each):

• Read career-related books:

_____
_____
_____
_____

• Volunteered in area of career interest:

_____
_____
_____
_____

• Watched videos/other media:

_____
_____
_____
_____

• Held job in area of career interest:

_____
_____
_____
_____

• Used computer to explore careers:

_____
_____
_____
_____

• Discussed career plans with parents/guardians:

_____
_____
_____
_____

• Interviewed people about their work:

_____
_____
_____
_____

• Talked with teacher/school counselor about my career plans:

_____
_____
_____
_____

• Job shadowed (observed someone at his or her job for several hours or more):

_____
_____
_____
_____

• Other career exploration activities:

_____
_____
_____
_____

## ACTIVITIES COMPLETED

Here you can keep a record of your progress in doing the activities for developing skills given in the chapters on Basic Skills, Thinking Skills, People Skills, and Personal Qualities. Write the activity number and the date you complete each activity on the lines provided.

## Basic Skills:

**READING**

| Activity Number | Date Completed |
|---|---|
| _____ | _____ |
| _____ | _____ |
| _____ | _____ |
| _____ | _____ |
| _____ | _____ |

**LISTENING**

| Activity Number | Date Completed |
|---|---|
| _____ | _____ |
| _____ | _____ |
| _____ | _____ |
| _____ | _____ |
| _____ | _____ |

**WRITING**

| | |
|---|---|
| _____ | _____ |
| _____ | _____ |
| _____ | _____ |
| _____ | _____ |
| _____ | _____ |

**SPEAKING**

| | |
|---|---|
| _____ | _____ |
| _____ | _____ |
| _____ | _____ |
| _____ | _____ |
| _____ | _____ |

**MATH**

| | |
|---|---|
| _____ | _____ |
| _____ | _____ |
| _____ | _____ |
| _____ | _____ |
| _____ | _____ |

THESE ARE MY SKILLS

## ACTIVITIES COMPLETED
*(Continued)*

## Thinking Skills:

### CREATIVE THINKING

| Activity Number | Date Completed |
|---|---|
| _____ | _____ |
| _____ | _____ |
| _____ | _____ |
| _____ | _____ |
| _____ | _____ |

### PROBLEM SOLVING

| | |
|---|---|
| _____ | _____ |
| _____ | _____ |
| _____ | _____ |
| _____ | _____ |
| _____ | _____ |

### DECISION MAKING

| Activity Number | Date Completed |
|---|---|
| _____ | _____ |
| _____ | _____ |
| _____ | _____ |
| _____ | _____ |
| _____ | _____ |

### VISUALIZATION

| | |
|---|---|
| _____ | _____ |
| _____ | _____ |
| _____ | _____ |
| _____ | _____ |
| _____ | _____ |

## People Skills:

### SOCIAL

| Activity Number | Date Completed |
|---|---|
| _____ | _____ |
| _____ | _____ |
| _____ | _____ |
| _____ | _____ |
| _____ | _____ |

### NEGOTIATION

| | |
|---|---|
| _____ | _____ |
| _____ | _____ |
| _____ | _____ |
| _____ | _____ |
| _____ | _____ |

### LEADERSHIP

| | |
|---|---|
| _____ | _____ |
| _____ | _____ |
| _____ | _____ |
| _____ | _____ |
| _____ | _____ |

### TEAMWORK

| Activity Number | Date Completed |
|---|---|
| _____ | _____ |
| _____ | _____ |
| _____ | _____ |
| _____ | _____ |
| _____ | _____ |

### CULTURAL DIVERSITY

| | |
|---|---|
| _____ | _____ |
| _____ | _____ |
| _____ | _____ |
| _____ | _____ |

## ACTIVITIES COMPLETED

*(Continued)*

## Personal Qualities:

**SELF-ESTEEM**

| ACTIVITY NUMBER | DATE COMPLETED |
|---|---|
| _____ | _____ |
| _____ | _____ |
| _____ | _____ |
| _____ | _____ |
| _____ | _____ |

**RESPONSIBILITY**

| ACTIVITY NUMBER | DATE COMPLETED |
|---|---|
| _____ | _____ |
| _____ | _____ |
| _____ | _____ |
| _____ | _____ |
| _____ | _____ |

**SELF-MANAGEMENT**

| | |
|---|---|
| _____ | _____ |
| _____ | _____ |
| _____ | _____ |
| _____ | _____ |
| _____ | _____ |

# Putting It All Together

I started this book with an invitation: I asked you to join with me in learning about job skills. I hope you are enjoying this journey and are as enthused about learning skills as I am. As I said at the beginning: "It's great to feel strong. Confident. Successful. And skills make these feelings possible."

Not only do skills give you these good feelings, they are essential for your future success. To work, you must have skills. For you to be paid by an employer, or to receive income from a business you own, you must have marketable skills.

Everyone needs the following Foundation Skills to succeed.

| | |
|---|---|
| Reading | Social Skills |
| Writing | Negotiation |
| Mathematics | Leadership |
| Speaking | Teamwork |
| Listening | Cultural Diversity |
| Creative Thinking | Self-Esteem |
| Problem Solving | Self-Management |
| Decision Making | Responsibility |
| Visualization | |

In addition to the Foundation Skills, you need Special Skills. You learned in this book how to identify these skills. In Chapter 5, you can assess your personality type and then find occupations that are likely to fit you. In Chapter 11, you can identify your motivated skills. Together, your personality type and your motivated skills can give you a career direction. They point the way to the Special Skills you can explore to see if you would enjoy learning and using them.

As you chart your future career direction, think of the people you met in this book, especially those who are "soaring to new heights." I think of those who did not let sex or race stereotypes limit their thinking, people like aquatic biologist JoAnn Burkholder and corporate executive Tom Jones. And weren't you impressed by the competence and confidence of James Benton? Being able to see was not necessary for him to succeed and excel. And what about Herbert and Virginia Dooley's dream of owning a cattle ranch? These individuals set goals, planned, worked hard, and took reasonable risks.

As you think ahead, think of the teens you met in this book, like Kai Cheng, Jennifer TenEyck, Diego Soria, and Jess Petrosky. They are excited about learning. They are moving out. For them, "The sky is the limit!"

At the beginning of this book, I asked you to keep four points in mind. Let's take another look at them.

1. *Many people want to help you.* You saw this throughout the book: Dwayne Patterson helping teens in the Raleigh Youth Council, and Barry Blystone showing Nicole Smith how to use electrical test equipment. Family members also want to help: parents, grandparents, uncles and aunts. Teachers, school counselors, and adults in the workplace also want to help.

   Reach out to them. Talk with them about their jobs. Share with them what you are learning, what you would like to learn. Talk with them about this book. Ask them for help.

2. *Real learning requires action.* Set goals for yourself and plan. Then, do it! Reread the section in Chapter 13 on goal setting and planning. Decide on what you want to learn. Is it one of the Foundation Skills? There are great activities for strengthening your skills in Chapters 6 through 9. There are many great ways to learn new skills in Chapter 14. And, then, keep a record—a job skills portfolio— just like Meredith in Chapter 16.

3. *You need to learn skills now to be ready for the future.* With the skills you learn this week, you will be more powerful next week. Brick by brick, skill by skill, you are building your future. Remember how Governor Jim Hunt built his self-confidence and skills? Gradually, step-by-step, over time.

4. *It's up to you.* You owe it to yourself to be an active skill learner. Learning skills will make you more curious, confident, and excited about life. Life will be more fun. You will be more interesting to be around. You will better understand yourself and the world around you.

Start today. Promise yourself that you will use what you read in this book. Set a reasonable goal. Work on it and keep a record. Reward yourself as you succeed. Record the results in your portfolio. Remember, "Today is the beginning of the rest of your life."

# Index

COMPILED BY KAY BANNING

Creative thinking skills
    activities completed, 198
    definition of, 26, 72
    importance of, 200
    improvement of, 74-75
    job interview form and, 30
    occupations using, 72-73
    problem-solving skills and, 74
    self-estimates for, 87
    as thinking skill, 20, 71-75
Cultural diversity skills
    activities completed, 198
    definition of, 26, 103
    development of, 104-06
    importance of, 19, 200
    job interview form and, 31
    occupations using, 103-04
    as people skill, 20, 102-06
    self-estimates of, 107

Day, Olivia, 168
*Dealing with Anger,* 94
Decision-making skills
    achieving dreams and, 160
    activities completed, 198
    decisional balance sheet, 81-82
    definition of, 26, 78
    importance of, 78, 200
    improvement of, 80-81
    job interview form and, 30
    occupations using, 79-80
    self-estimates for, 87
    as thinking skill, 20, 78-82
Decisional balance sheet, 81-82
Degele, John F., 182
Denkler-Rainey, Patricia, 147-49
Dew, Bettie, 121-22
Dextré, Abelardo, 133-34
Díaz, Lope Max, 89
Dooley, Herbert, 160-61, 201
Dooley, Virginia, 160-61, 201
Douville, Patsy, 54-55
Dreams. *See also* Careers; Goal-setting skills
    achieving, 157-65
    creating your future, 157-58
    goal-setting skills and, 161-64
    job skills and, 159
    planning skills and, 164
    self-management skills and, 160
    sexual involvement, postponement of, 158-59
    steps to reaching, 159-61
    stereotypes and, 145-53
    working after school and, 165

Earnings, 13-14, 23, 200
Education. *See also* Skills development
    academic program, 191-92, 194
    cooperative education, 178
    after high school, 179-85, 192, 195
    school activities and, 168-69
    school-to-work transition programs, 174-78
    success and, 4
    tech prep, 178, 181
    vocational and technical, 176-77
    working after school, 165
Ellis, A., 110
Ellis, Albert, 114
Employment, 7-16, 165. *See also* Careers; Job security; Occupations
*Encyclopedia of Career Change and Work Issues,* 110, 114
*Encyclopedia of Careers and Vocational Guidance,* 48, 131
Enterprising personality type, 34, 35, 43-44, 140-41
Exide Electronics, 9, 21-23, 52, 99, 121

Farnham, Brent, 83
*Feeling Good,* 114
Foundation skills. *See also* Basic skills; People skills; Personal qualities skills; Thinking skills
    definition of, 20, 26
    identifying, 24
    importance of, 23, 25, 53, 200
    job interview form and, 29-32
    in job skills portfolio, 86, 192
    as marketable skills, 21
    short-term goals and, 163
    vocational and technical education and, 176
    worker interviews and, 27-28
4H, and learning new skills, 169-71
Four-year college, 180
Frequency count, and goals, 164
Fucile, Rose, 146

Goal-setting skills, 120, 160-64, 166-67, 191. *See also* Dreams; Self-management skills
*GOE (Guide for Occupational Exploration),* 45, 48, 130, 180
Graduation, plans after high school, 179-85, 192, 195
Graham, Patty, 95
Grannan, Nick, 168
Graphs, 61
Greene, Sandra, 92
Gross pay, 13. See also Pay
*Guide for Occupational Exploration (GOE),* 45, 48, 130, 180

Hayes, Alphonso, 79, 147
Helms, Jackson, 193